NOTE FROM AUTHOR:

Business ownership is most definitely not for everyone; it is my wish to ass[i]
efficient, informative and engaging fashion - if it is or is not the right path f

So many of my clients started without the means to make a conscious cho
them are doing well, they have struggled. Doing many of the exercises contained in this boo[k]
enabled them to understand why they struggled with certain aspects, to appreciate their strengths
and weaknesses, and to make better choices both for themselves and their business.

I believe that anyone can be a great business owner, in their own way, if they make themselves self-
aware, structure accordingly and remain true to themselves. 'It's All About You' is designed to
enable you to learn a lot about yourself, in a structured fashion, so that you can objectively assess if
you are ready, and what you're ready for, when it comes to owning and running a business.

Some of this book will be theoretical and I ask you stick with it; I share the theory to enable you to
educate yourself in order to gain a better understanding of yourself. Within the book will be
exercises, some require you just to think, others are more interactive – I ask that you take the
appropriate time to give them due effort. They are only useful if they are approached with an open-
mind and completed with honest integrity.

As you progress through this book, I want you to keep remembering these three key things:

1) There is no right answer, just be true to yourself
2) What you want from your business is entirely personal – don't expect your answer to be the
   same as anyone else's
3) Being a business owner is multi-faceted - it's about you, your customers, making a
   difference, providing for your family, a lifestyle, a legacy – some or all of these things and
   many others.

I am dedicating this book to my dad, who became a business owner in the late 80s at the height of a
recession, and nearly 30 years later has been through many trials and tribulations, and upon reading
this book said, "I wish I'd had this back in 1989 when I started…." So for all those now standing in my
dad's shoes, I sincerely hope this helps you assess and make the decision that's right for you…

Charlotte

It's All About You © 2021 – A Trading name of Conscious Action Ltd – Company No: 8227151 – VAT: 151 6932 11

TABLE OF CONTENTS

OUTCOMES

THIS BOOK WILL TEACH YOU:

- ➢ What being a business owner means – the role and responsibilities
- ➢ What behaviours, skills and attitudes are best to fulfil that role
- ➢ To assess if you really want to be a business owner
- ➢ To clarify and articulate what you want your business to deliver for you, your clients and humanity
- ➢ To prepare mentally and psychologically for the planning process ahead, using Integral Theory

BY THE END YOU WILL:

- ➢ Have clarity regarding your suitability for being a business owner
- ➢ Understand how "starting with you" allows you to create a framework that is integral to the success of your business plan
- ➢ Have learnt the basics of Integral Theory and the importance of having all four quadrants aligned
- ➢ Understand what your personal value hierarchy is, what your career anchor is and your current behavioural profile, and how that manifests in you as a business owner
- ➢ Have completed practical exercises to identify and then exorcise any psychological barriers around abundance, success, money and capability.
- ➢ Have learnt some new tools to help you manifest all you have learnt throughout your business and the means to refresh and maintain it

GUIDANCE ON COMPLETING THIS BOOK:

This book is designed to make you think differently, to challenge the way you approach the basic fundamentals of business by gaining a deeper understanding of yourself.

As such, there may well be aspects of the book and exercises that will initially be challenging, and I ask you to stick with it, dig deep and be honest with yourself.

All the exercises and theories shared here are established, proven techniques that create breakthroughs and drive success.

All the exercises are available in written form at the end of the book, or you can download them from the web, where all other links and referred to items are curated for your ease of consumption. Please go to www.iaay.uk/resources to access or download.

To keep us focused and on track, in some cases I have extracted a specific part rather than share the whole more complicated approach.

If anything piques your interest, I'll happily share more with you. If anything really just makes you feel stuck, then please reach out for help.

WHAT IS A BUSINESS OWNER?

In business, clarity is your friend. The clearer you can be, the easier it will be to assess at each decision point which option takes you in the direction you want to go. Therefore, before we get into assessing your capabilities and preparedness to be a business owner, I want first to address what a business owner really is.

Terms these days can get used and interchanged in a variety of ways, and this can cause confusion. In the realm of business ownership, the terms you most likely hear are entrepreneur, start-up founder, small business owner, sole trader or self-employed. Are they all the same? What's the difference?

Well there are different ways to look at this. Some of these are legal definitions based on the type of business entity you have started.

Self-employed and sole trader fall into these categories. But we won't be looking at the legal stuff in this book

Start-up founder, whilst the term is technically defined as: 'someone who establishes an organisation', it is more commonly a term that's been synonymous with the high-tech market, where innovation linked with new technologies opened up a whole new market (think Google, Facebook, Apple). We are again, not really dealing with that here.

Sometimes I really do find it useful to say what things are not, as much as to say what they are…

So that leaves entrepreneur and business owner. Let us begin by exploring if they are the same thing.

BUSINESS OWNER VERSUS ENTREPRENEUR

In essence they are the same - someone who is the creator, owner and manager of a business, for the purpose of growth.

At the start I'd argue there is very little difference – both need significant hard work and dedication, but maybe over time the differences become more apparent…

THE PRIMARY DIFFERENCE BETWEEN BUSINESSES OWNERSHIP & ENTREPRENEURS [1]

- Business owners tend to deal with known and established business models and/or products & services – the more innovative and model-breaking the business, the more entrepreneurial
- Business owners often aim for limited growth and continued profitability to support lifestyle choices, while entrepreneurs target rapid growth and high productivity returns, but bore quickly – so create, grow, sell and start again….
- Business owners deal with risks for sure, but they tend to be more known and established risks. As entrepreneurs are challenging the current conventions, they tend to encounter unknown risks (note, this does not mean they are bigger or greater risk takers)

- Business owners want to make a difference, but they may have a smaller reach in mind, they set out to change their lives and those of customers and colleagues. Whereas entrepreneurs are focused more disrupting economies and humanity in a significant manner.

It's really about scale and intent – the day-to-day role and responsibilities are very similar – so I use it as nomenclature only.

SO THEN, WHAT DOES BEING A BUSINESS OWNER REALLY MEAN?

Definitions are few and far between, but in essence I like describing a business owner as:

"A business owner is someone who owns a business, either of product or service, with the aim of meeting a need in exchange for profit."

The type of business can vary hugely, the intent behind the business can be as diverse as the owners, but the basic concept is about exchange – you fulfil a need for your customer and in return they pay you.

WHAT IS THE ROLE DESCRIPTION – WHAT ARE THE RESPONSIBILITIES?

If we were to create a short job description for a business owner it would probably entail something around providing solutions to challenges and contributing positively to the economy of the country by providing private sector employment opportunities. It would almost definitely mention providing entrepreneurial skills with which to find solutions to new challenges or improve on an already discovered solution to a challenge. Simply put, business owners are innovators.

Business owners are expected to have a good knowledge of the market/industry they are venturing into, and must also understand the relationship between the business and the needs of the society, as well as those of their targeted clients or customers.

In order to succeed, the business owner must have a thorough understanding of the market, competitors, their customer needs, operational factors and have worked out a way to support the business to succeed (i.e. a plan).

A business owner works with a group of people he/she employs or partners with to carry out the purpose of the business. As such, they have the responsibility to understand the importance of the team they work with and conduct themselves in a trustworthy, ethical fashion, be that in respect to those they hire, outsource to or partner with. Even if you're a sole-trader you are never an island.

Ensuring they have the right team around them can be crucial to success and, as the leader, it is the duty of the business owner to ensure cohesive and coherent relationships between members of the team for it to work effectively.

Also, the progress, aim, and the day-to-day running of the business is part of the duty of the business owner. What that entails will of course largely depend on the type of business they run – services differ massively to products, online to offline, B2C and B2B require different approaches and a marketplace product requires both – hence knowledge of the specific environment is oh so crucial!

To bring this point to life, let's look at this role in terms of a job description; needless to say it makes no sense to have one, but a clear definition will help illustrate the key components of the role.

BUSINESS OWNER EXAMPLE JOB DESCRIPTION

Business owners perform various duties, tasks, and responsibilities geared towards making a success of their business, including:

- Articulating the vision, purpose and journey for the business
- Creating and maintaining the business plan and associated commercial budgets
- Ensuring appropriate resources and skillset are engaged to guarantee success
- Creating and implementing the sales and marketing strategies in line with the ideal target clients
- Putting in place the required operating model to support the vision, sales strategy and fulfilment needs
- Setting realistic but stretching targets/goals that are measurable and reported
- Regularly reviewing the plans and making adjustments as necessary (based on measureable feedback, income or challenges)
- Problem-solving any challenges that arise internally or externally, in a way that best serves both business and customer
- Foster a culture of proactivity, continuous improvement and coherence across both employees, partners and clients
- Proactively manage the finances and legal aspects of the business to ensure that ethically the business is robust, honest and safe
- Communicating openly, honestly and regularly to all involved to ensure consistency of message, culture and to celebrate success or overcome obstacles

And breathe!!

That can all be summarised neatly into a simple, if not slightly facetious, answer of: Everything! You name it, when you start a business it's all on you!

Strategy, planning, finance, legal, marketing, sales, customer service, operations, human resources to name but a few aspects of the business you will need to understand and look after. To say the buck stops with you is an understatement. Often this is the case because there is literally no one else, especially at these early stages of planning and starting a business. You may have 'sounding boards' in your friends and family, former colleagues, or maybe even a business coach or mentor (either hired or an established relationship with someone you already know) and of course there is always Google, but ultimately all decisions are yours and yours alone.

This means you need to be prepared for all that may come, and understand these demands and requirements, and if you have what is required to be able to make a sustainable business.

Ultimately, as time progresses you will (hopefully) hire people to take on various aspects of your business and so you can tailor your role to your skillset and desire:

- Maybe you're a practitioner and want someone else to do the business part so you can just be with the clients

- Maybe you're a salesperson through and through and need to delegate the operations side of the business
- Maybe you are the teacher or facilitator and you need sales people
- Maybe you love public speaking, and want others to run the events and see clients one-to-one while you deliver your message to big crowds

All of these variations are viable, but at the start you need to be able to at least understand the importance of what 'good' looks like and how to do every aspect of the business to a satisfactory level to get you off the ground. To be clear, it is not about money. You may be able to pay people from the outset, but that doesn't alter the responsibility; you still need to ensure you understand and can manage all these aspects.

BEING A BUSINESS OWNER IS A BIG RESPONSIBILITY AND PLAINLY SAID: IT'S NOT FOR EVERYONE! BUT HOW DO YOU ASSESS IF IT IS FOR YOU?

Well luckily for us, there are lots of very intelligent and dedicated researchers out there that can help us with this very question.

So we're going to take a deep look at the personality traits and skillsets that are most common amongst business owners, and look at some exercises to assess if you are that type of person (or can take on the traits to become so).

Let's begin with a piece of research that I really like as it's the summary research study called the 'Big Five Personality Dimensions and Entrepreneurial Status Study' [2], which looked at 23 studies and explored the differences between business owners and managers in the corporate environment. As many people looking to start a business are currently employed in the corporate world, this seems like an excellent comparison to use. Does being an excellent manager make you a good business owner?

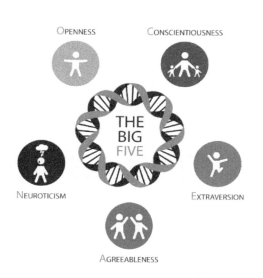

If we take this work and the Five Dimensions and translate them into normal speak (so to speak), then we can say that four major factors for business owners are:

1) **It's not about job security; it's about building something**

Most business owners are hoping their business will create an opportunity for economic independence. It's not uncommon for a business owner to leave the security of a 'good job' to start their business. Research shows that up to half follow their passion, go out on their own and are willing to put their own money behind it (either personal savings and/or personal credit to get things off the ground.). This relates to Extraversion, Conscientiousness and Openness to Experience

2) It's about something bigger than themselves or the business

Creating a legacy, changing humanity or the world, is often a driver. Again, across a range of surveys 80% reference 'giving back' as a driver. Very often the inspiration for a business comes from a personal slight – something the owner suffered, something that irritates them about a product or service they love, a bad experience, a sector of society that is neglected. We'll come back to this later as it's a key piece to understand before you move forward. This relates to Openness to Experience and Agreeableness

3) It might not be easy, but they say it's worth it

Running a business can be very rewarding, but it's not for everyone—there are easier ways to make a living. Is all the hard work and sacrifice worth it? It sounds like it. 90% of survey respondents say they would do it again and 65% say they are better off financially than if they'd remained someone else's employee. This relates to Conscientiousness and Neuroticism

4) Getting to work is a way of life

People looking for a '9 to 5' job don't typically start their own businesses. Business owners work longer hours – if they ever stop. In many surveys, over 67% report working during the weekends even if their businesses aren't open for business at the weekend. 80% admitted to taking work home and it's not uncommon for those with families to jump back into work for a few hours after everyone else in the family has gone to bed. This relates to Conscientiousness and Agreeableness and Neuroticism

Basically, many business owners don't ever unplug. They are 'all in' when it comes to doing whatever it takes to be successful.

NO RISK TAKING?

When you think of a successful business owner, which personality traits do you think of?

For many, the media has conjured images of someone who has risked it all to pursue their passion. Someone who quits their 'day job', sleeps on friends' couches, works out of a garage, eats noodles or toast for breakfast, lunch and dinner, sacrificing comfort, security and even stability all in the name of dedication and commitment. There is no safety net, no backup plan; they are literally 'all in', because, after all, pressure breeds efficiency and ingenuity, right? Think Elon Musk, or Steve Jobs.

Well, yes – although they are most definitely the exception, not the rule!

The notion of the risk-loving business owner who gives it all up to take a giant leap of faith into the unknown is further from the truth than you may think. This is a good thing, especially when you consider the hard, bleak truth that nine out of every ten start-ups will fail. In actuality, the evidence suggests that entrepreneurs may lean the other way when it comes to risk.

I will make a differentiation here, if you want to get into the world of tech start-ups then this is not the process for you. The technology industry is so fast moving, and so dominated that a different set of rules apply. If that's the area you want to explore, then whilst this book will definitely be helpful in really understanding yourself, it's not aimed at you.

Back to non-tech businesses then... In his book, 'Originals: How Non-Conformists Move the World', Adam Grant (an organisational psychologist) argues that successful business owners are not the extreme risk-takers we often imagine them to be, but rather the more conservative individuals who are more apt, not less, to hedge their bets. It's characteristics of flexibility, and conscientiousness that when combined together may appear to be risk-taking, but are actually methodically thought through conscious choices.

INSPIRATIONAL VISIONARIES?

But Business Owners are inspirational right? The media is full of examples of entrepreneurial business owners that were so successful they became household names – like Richard Branson at Virgin, Tony Hsieh at Zappos, Lisa Stone at BlogHer, Blake Mycoskie at Toms, or Katrina Mountanos at Manicube.

Firstly, not everyone wants that kind of success; remember, world domination is not the only dream. Some just want to be able to work 3-days a week and still afford their mortgage, or just want to make the world a better place. Personally, I'm pretty inspired by Taylor Conroy [3] and weJourney.co – check out his story by going to the resource page and choosing his video there: iaay.uk/resources

Whatever your chosen reality is; that's a great dream too.

Returning to the earlier points about the differences between business owners and entrepreneurs, not everyone has the skillset and drive to change society to that degree so let's not look at the exceptions; there are thousands upon thousands of successful business owners who, contrary to conventional wisdom, do not possess Type A Personality traits (overachieving, hyper-organised workaholic or an extrovert).

The best business owners do however share a collection of characteristics and exhibit a specific range of behaviours. We will now explore these and provide you with some practical exercises to assist you in deciding if business ownership is for you.

Throughout this section of the book you'll notice nine boxes, each one detailing a key characteristic, along with examples of how that may manifest in a successful business owner. Make sure you read and reflect on each...

Characteristics: (spaced out around the book section)

There may be a hundred remarkable character and personality traits that define you or your favourite successful small business owner. When you compare these traits, a handful of key traits rise to the top.

Tenacity/ Resilience/ Drive
Starting a business is an ultramarathon. You have to be able to live with uncertainty and push through a crucible of obstacles. Business owners who can avoid giving up have a better chance of

finding their market and outlasting their inevitable mistakes. This trait is known by many names - perseverance, persistence, determination, commitment, resilience.

Most small business owners are driven to succeed; they want to see their businesses grow, from start-up to established business. Tenacity is therefore a very common characteristic because starting a business is challenging, and some challenges call for a moderate amount of competitiveness, determination and motivation.

Being a small business owner comes with its up and downs; there are victories, setbacks, chaos and calm waters. The most successful are those who are resilient and able to bounce back after an unexpected challenge and get back up after facing a setback.

Passion
All successful business owners have found a passion that takes them beyond the simple profit and loss. Most will tell how they are fuelled by a passion for their product or service, by the opportunity to solve a problem and make life easier, better or cheaper.

"Most entrepreneurs I know believe they will change the world," says Jay Friedlander, a professor of sustainable business who works with entrepreneurs at the College of the Atlantic and at Babson College. "There's an excitement and belief in what they're doing that gets them through the hard times." It can be very difficult to overcome the challenges of starting and running a successful business without a true passion for your work. Some of the most successful small business owners have either directly developed businesses based on their passions, or they are able to incorporate things they are passionate about into the day-to-day operation of their businesses.

Tolerance of Ambiguity
This classic trait is the definition of risk-taking - the ability to withstand the fear of uncertainty and potential failure. The ability to control fear is the most important trait of all. Fear of humiliation, fear of missing payroll, running out of cash, bankruptcy, the list goes on.

This is where the ultimate test takes place, on the mental battlefield. You can go with the fear and quit, or push through it. We have the power to control our thoughts. When we commit mentally, our action follows. While many would feel powerless in the face of such adversity, the successful business owner looks at the situation and knows they have some control over the outcome.

Vision with Focus
One of the defining traits is the ability to spot an opportunity and imagine something where others have not. A curiosity that identifies overlooked niches and puts them at the forefront of innovation and emerging fields. They imagine another world and have the ability to communicate that vision effectively.

Business owners need to handle a vast array of responsibilities in their businesses, wearing many different hats during the course of the workday. The ability to block out distractions and focus on the immediate issue, task or goal, as well as maintain the connection to their vision can be a key trait.

Self-Belief/ Confidence

Self-confidence is a key trait. You have to be resolutely certain that your product or service is something the world/market/client needs and that you can deliver it to overcome the naysayers, (who, by the way, will always deride what the majority has yet to validate). Researchers define this trait as task-specific confidence. It's a belief that turns the risk proposition around - you've conducted enough research and have enough confidence that you can get the job done that you ameliorate the risk.

Confidence is a very powerful character trait that can instil trust, facilitate respect, and often lead to increased success. The most successful business owners have a steady, quiet confidence that doesn't border on arrogance or egotism.

Flexible and Open-Minded

Business survival, like that of the species, depends on adaptation. Your final product or service almost definitely won't look anything like what you started with. Flexibility that allows you to respond to changing tastes and market conditions is essential. Often this is the hardest thing to do, after nurturing your business, is to then time to 'let your baby go'. Being open to taking criticism and feedback, and still being able to see the vision through the adaptions is a crucial skill. Whilst focus is an important trait found in most successful business owners, it's also important to keep an open mind and consider different perspectives. Business owners who are willing to consider alternative ideas and try new processes may be more likely to reach significant levels of success.

Goal-Oriented Continuous Improvement

Tenacity can take a small business owner far, provided there is a defined target to be reached. Without SMART goals and the ability to focus on the actions required to reach those goals, success can be elusive. Most successful business owners take time to set goals so they have clarity about where they are going and how they intend to get there. They also make sure that those goals are measurable, and that they regularly review them in order to ensure that their goals are taking them in the intended direction and that they are capturing all the learning to date.

Self-Reliant but Humble

Many business owners need to start out as totally self-reliant. The ability to think and act independently, without the input of others, is a required trait in the early stages, and common among successful business owners. Whilst being self-reliant is useful, the most successful are also able to ask for help when they need it, give credit where credit is due, admit when they are wrong, and accept constructive criticism. These business owners have an ability to keep their feet on the ground during even the most satisfying accomplishment, and never forget where they started from.

Commercially Minded

Since a significant part of business success can be related to financial success, most successful business owners become very savvy at budgeting and sticking to a set budget as they manage the operation of their businesses. The ability to know what funds you have available, where to reduce expenses, and how to make smart decisions when it comes to spending, can often determine the success of a small business.

EXERCISE 1: BEHAVIOURAL PROFILE

If you'd like to see if you naturally have the behaviours that are needed at this stage of the business start-up journey, then a great model to use is the Schroder's Behavioural Model [4]. You may have already done this as it's a freebie exercise, I give away to introduce the book. If so, great, you can recap; if not then let me introduce it to you as Harold Schroder and Tony Cockerill's Model of Behaviours is one of the most respected and validated behavioural models around.

The model comprises of 11 discrete behaviours, each of which enable individuals to perform at outstanding levels in an unpredictable, complex and fast changing environment (which starting a business most definitely is).

It is possible to both measure and learn these behaviours, making them an ideal framework to use for someone considering a change in their approach to their career.

By utilising an example profile, that would best reflect a new business owner starting up a business, and some detailed competency descriptions and attainment statements I will provide you, you can complete a self-assessment to ascertain where your strengths lie in comparison to the profile.

This process will help you see what your current strengths are, and where your limitations are. This is crucial to be aware of and to reflect upon, relative to what is needed at this stage of the journey. You can then assess dispassionately if you want, and are willing, to work on the areas of limitation and to be mindful of finding partners or support in those areas too.

If you've already started your business, then please get in touch and we can look at alternative profiles for you.

TAKE A LOOK AT THEM...

The behaviours fall into four (4) clusters: Imagine, Involve, Ignite and Improve, which reflect the lifecycle of any task – and essentially running a business is simply completing a never ending task list....

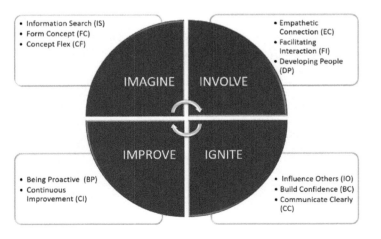

Here are the standard definitions for each of the 11 Behaviours:

Cluster	Behaviour	Definition
Imagine	Information Search (IS)	Gathers many different kinds of information and uses a wide variety of sources to build a rich informational environment in preparation for decision-making
	Forming Concepts (FC)	Builds frameworks or models or forms concepts; hypotheses an idea on the basis of information; becomes aware of patterns; trends and cause/effort relations by linking disparate information
	Conceptual Flexing (CF)	Identifies feasible alternatives or multiple options in planning and decision-making; holds different options in focus simultaneously and evalates their pros and cons
Involve	Empathetic Connection (EC)	Uses open and probing questions; summarises, paraphrasing etc to understand ideas, concepts and feelings of another; can comprehend events, issues, problems and opportunities from the viewpoint of others
	Facilitating Interaction (FI)	Involes others and is able to build co-operative teams in which group members feel valued and empowered and have shared goals
	Developing People (DP)	Creates a positive climate in which staff increase the accuracy of their awareness of their own strenths and limitations; provides coachig, training and developmental resources to improve performance
Ignite	Influencing Others (IO)	Uses a variety of methods (e.g. persuasive arguments, modelling behaviours, inventing symbols, forming alliances and appealing to the interest of others) to gain support for ideas and strategies and values
	Building Confidence (BC)	States own "stand" or position on issues, unhesitatingly takes decisions when required and commits self and others accordingly; expresses confidence in the future success of the actions to be taken
	Communicating Clearly (CC)	Presents ideas clearly, with ease and interest so that the other person (or audience) understands what is being communicated; uses technical, symbolic and non-verbal language and visual aids effectively
Improve	Being Proactive (BP)	Structures the tasks for the team; implements plans and ideas; takes responsbility for all aspects of the situation even beyond ordinary boundaries - and for the success and failure of the group
	Continuous Improvement (CI)	Posesses high internal work standards and sets ambitious, risky and yet attainable goals; wants to do things better, to improve, to be more effective and efficient; measures progress against targets.

Each of the 11 behaviours has been defined and then articulated against a set of standardised 1-5 level descriptions. We can use this to estimate your current personal behavioural profile.

As we said, the model involves a 1-5 rating system that is based on deviation away from adequacy (level 3).

In the below diagram you can see the generic model with the variances explained as they are in the original model.

To the left you will see the names given to the levels in the exercise that we are about to do. I have also corresponded the colours for your ease.

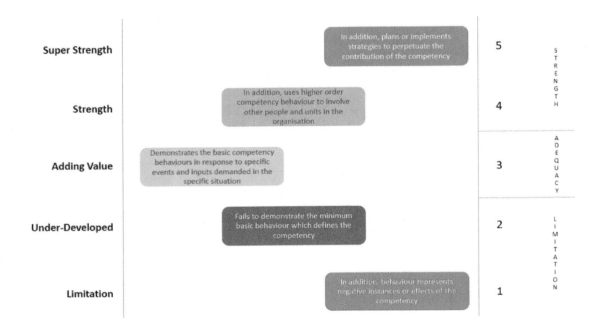

Ideally each individual should expect to excel (level 5) in say, four (4) areas, but we would want to ensure their team covers all 11 areas. Therefore, another benefit in completing this exercise is that it will help you assess what strengths you want to look for in business partners, team members or your support team. Which four (4) will vary, and different roles would ideally require certain behaviours to be stronger than others. For this exercise I've prepared a guide profile that I find best represents the needs at the start of the journey.

Each behaviour then has statements describing how it is measurably evidenced at each of those five levels - ranging from negative use of the behaviour at level one (Limitation), to an inspirational use of the behaviour at level five (Super Strength).

Traditionally, to assess these levels you'd use real-life situational observations, or you'd ask people who regularly work with you to complete it (commonly called a 360 review). However, for the purposes of this exercise I am going to ask you to self-assess. We will then use the guide profile that is reflective of the behavioural needs of a 'typical' small business owner at the start of the business journey, to give you something to reflect on.

SHALL WE GET INTO THE DETAIL NOW?

To do that you need to download the excel spreadsheet, which contains the level statements for each behaviour, and the profile that we will now go through together.

The exercise is available from the iaay website—you need to download the exercises: iaay.uk/resources

Complete Your Behaviour Profile

We are going to take this in five steps.

STEP 1: ASSESSING IMAGINE CLUSTER

 In all the research that sits behind this work, it was evident that at least 95% of businesses fell at this first hurdle – the Imagine Cluster. Having inadequate levels of behaviour here lead to uninformed thinking and decision taken without adequate rationale. When starting a business there are so many types of information you need to consider, so many variables to factor in, that this is a key cluster to ensure you start your business off with a good chance for success.

So let's look at each of the behaviours and understand how it manifests at this stage of the business lifecycle. And what questions you should ask yourself when looking to assess.

- **Information Search –**
  How effectively do you explore and seek out information necessary to progress the design, idea or task at hand? Be that competitor or market information, operational solutions, branding options, selecting an accountant to go with etc.

- **Forming Concepts –**
  Are you capable of creating or evolving your ideas from synthesising information to turning it into a workable solution? - Science's interaction with your dream/gut feeling…

To many, their business idea is like a baby – perfect just as it is… I would estimate that 100% of businesses never end up as they started. To go on this journey, you are going to need to be willing to take on information that contradicts your gut, assess it and, where appropriate, discard it or incorporate it… this behaviour is key for that.

- **Concept Flexing –** How well can you develop a range of ideas, while at the same time ensuring you don't become too narrow-minded, fixed or stuck on just one? Your business is your baby, but that doesn't mean it stays the same from conception through to reality…

Now go to the spreadsheet, take a look at the Statement tab and read the level 1-5 descriptions of these three behaviours. Take time to reflect on situations you've been in, which can be work or social (our behaviours don't tend to change that much between the two). I always find as I read each level description an example comes to mind – someone that I feel epitomises that level – sometimes that makes me laugh or smile, other times it's an 'aha' moment explaining those frustrating times.

I've indicated the level that a typical business owner at this stage would ideally be at to enable them to have the best chance of success. These are indicated by the blue boxes filled in against each statement.

It's your turn now, having reflected, and with honest intent, answer the question:

Which level most commonly describes your approach?

Be honest!! We know we all have variances – good days, bad days, 'shouldn't have gotten out of bed' days, and we all know how we'd 'like' to think we operate (level five on everything all day every day). Leave all that at the door and trust your gut and be honest – rate yourself in the purple 'You' box.

STEP 2: ASSESSING THE INVOLVE CLUSTER

No man is an island, and whilst being a business owner means the buck stops with you, it actually means you need support, expertise and a team more than you ever did before. Sometimes that's friends and family, others a technical skill or knowledge expert. So whilst some of the descriptions may be slightly too 'corporate' or out of place for a start-up with maybe only you – it is all still relevant.

Let's look at the behaviours here:

- ***Empathetic Connection***
  Can you listen and playback others' perspectives and create deep connection, understanding and engagement? Are you able to be objective about your business? Are you able to listen to the expertise of others on areas of business that are not your forte?

- ***Facilitating Interaction***
  Can you effectively support and encourage genuine connection and interaction between the group? It may be your business, but it will require a team effort to get it going; even when it's just suppliers or tech support, everyone will need a shared vision, and to work together (family and friends count here too by the way).

- ***Developing People***
  Can you effectively guide the development of others through support? Those that work with you on this will want to get something out of it too, and your dream realisation probably won't do it for them? So what are you giving them? Advancement, experience, status, kudos, responsibility? These all count and sometimes delegation (*true delegation*) is your best friend as a business owner.

It's that time again – back to the spreadsheet and read the behaviour statements for the Involve Cluster. Once again I've added the Business Owner Guide Profile and once again I ask you to read, reflect and be honest. Your assessment in the 'You' purple box please.

I'm going to use a dirty word here – sales. Regardless of your type of business, and regardless of your personality, every business owner has an aspect of sales to their role. Or rather, they all have the responsibility to tell their story. In the 'It's All About You' book we look in depth at this aspect of being a business owner. We explore why, from a psychological perspective, the reason you're doing something and your ability to communicate that is the key to engaging your audience. These are the behaviours therefore that you need to excel at here at the start of the business lifecycle. Let's look at why...

- *Influencing Others*
  How capable are you of building partnerships with those people necessary to achieve the outcomes you desire? How capable are you of influencing those people and yourself to take action? You are going to need help, and you are going to need them to come on the journey with you. Can you find the win:win outcomes that will enable that?

- *Building Confidence*
  How well can you create belief, inspiration and certainty in the ability to accomplish the goals, projects and ideas? No-one wants to follow a leader who lacks certainty. This applies to yourself, in terms of self-confidence, as much as it does to those around you, both in your personal life to support you and in the professional arena to go on this journey with you. Some decisions will be outside your comfort zone - so delegate or trust but, whichever you choose to do, do it with confidence!

- *Communicating Clearly*
  Can you clearly and compellingly communicate the plan to yourself and others? Whether it's explaining it to a web designer, articulating yourself in an article or selling it to an investor, you have to be able to tell your story, get your vision across confidently, clearly and succinctly.

Taking a look at the spreadsheet once again, you will see that I've rated all of these Behaviours as 5 (Super Strength) for a business owner.

As previously stated, we'd ideally expect four behaviours at this level and here is where we see these coming into their own. Being able to take people on your journey is key at this fundamentally important phase. As we progress more into the planning and launching of the business that adjusts slightly – but for now, it's read, reflect, be honest and rate yourself.

So far we've looked a lot at what you might argue are the softer, more touchy-feely types of behaviours. Well this cluster is all about getting real, and getting stuff done. Many people under estimate how much is actually involved in the admin side of being a business owner – the marketing, the sales, fulfilment, accounting, operations etc. Many of which you may not necessarily enjoy or be good at, so these two behaviours are key; many more business fails than succeed. I believe these are two of the reasons why.

STARTUP FAILURE RATE STATISTICS

- *Slightly over 50% of small businesses <u>fail</u> in the first four years.*
  Leading <u>causes</u> of small business failure:
  - *Incompetence: 46%;*
  - *Unbalanced experience or lack of managerial experience: 30%;*
  - *Lack of experiences in line of goods or services: 11%.*

So, let's examine exactly what these last two behaviours are, and how they manifest in this context:

- **Being Proactive**
  How disciplined are you at driving initiatives forward, making things happen and removing obstacles to action or success? Starting a business takes work, and the to do list gets longer and longer - You need to be organised (realistically so), self-motivated, task-orientated and driven by the passion for your idea to get it off the ground.

- **Continuous Improvement**
  How focused are you on enhancing the effectiveness and efficiency of your strategy and approach based on feedback from measuring results? Many small business fail because they are inefficient - burning money and time unconsciously. Even from the start, you need to be looking for improvement - not at the expense of getting something out there (perfectionism has no place here), but also not at the expense of resources...

So for the final time, let's go to the spreadsheet, read, reflect, be honest and rate. Step 5: Create your Profile

So taking the 1-5 scores for each of the behaviours, now go to the Profile Tab where (if you've followed the instructions correctly) your answers will have been transposed to create a bar graph against the guide profile I've been recommending. It should look something like the example below:

Reflect on this for a while; acknowledge where your strengths (be they natural or learnt and cultivated) from your experience to date reside. Celebrate these strengths!

Try not to beat yourself up if you notice a large discrepancy between where I've said the business owner profile ideally is and where you've rated yourself. These can be learnt; so great, we've just created the development plan for you!

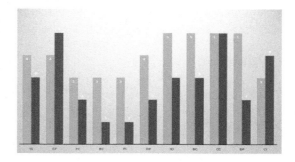

Exercise 2: Schein Career Anchor Theory [5]

Career anchor theory deals with the choices adults make in their careers based on the major motivational forces that drive them. Career anchor theory focuses on the 'internal' career, the career as experienced by the career occupant. It focuses on how motivation, competence, and values gradually combined to create a 'self-concept' that constrains and determines career choices. People with different career anchors desire different kinds of work settings, and are motivated by different kinds of incentives and rewards, etc

The theory was created by Edgar Schein in the 1970s. He's now the Head Professor of the MIT Sloan Management Institute and has been at the forefront of organisational and career psychology for almost 50 years. During the 1970s his research resulted in the creation of five (and later eight) career anchors

His definition of a career anchor is *a self-concept consisting of:*

> ➢ *our self-perceived talents and abilities,*
> ➢ *our self-perceived attitudes and values*

and, most importantly:

> ➢ *our self-perceived sense of motives and needs (which evolve over time and via experience)*

The first two concepts are based on actual experience in a work setting, while the third is derived from the individual's reaction to a variety of norms and values encountered in different social and work situations.

Career anchors only evolve as one gains occupational and life experience. However, once the self-concept has been formed, it functions as a stabilising force, hence the metaphor of an 'anchor', and can be thought of as the values and motives that the person will **not** give up if forced to make a choice.

Most of us are not aware of our career anchors until we are forced to make choices pertaining to self-development, family, or career. Considering if becoming a business owner is right for you is the perfect time to factor in your career anchors. All can lead to successful businesses; this is more about acknowledging it and ensuring you factor it into your planning...

According to Schein, when individuals achieve congruence between their career anchor and their work, they are more likely to attain positive career outcomes, such as job effectiveness, satisfaction, and stability. So knowing what you are anchored by, and therefore constructing your business to support that is going to be a better way to achieve what you want.

So What are they?

General Managerial	Entrepreneurial Creativity	Service or Dedication to a Cause	Pure Challenge
• Want to be a manager – seen as a metric of success • Natural problem–solvers even in conditions of uncertainty and ambiguity • People-people – have the ability to influence, supervise and lead effectively. • Emotional competent - stimulated by emotional and interpersonal crises. • Thrive on responsibility and can manage the politics and emotions.	• These people like to invent, be creative and run their own businesses. • They get bored easily and can be unpractical in their creativity • Wealth is their metric of success • Their overarching need is for whatever they build or create to be entirely their own – ownership is very important. • They differ from the Autonomous though, as they are more than willing to share the workload	• Service-orientated people care more about how they can help people than using their talents. • Interested in providing solutions in areas that have an exponentially larger impact. • Willing to withstand challenge and hardship in the pursuit of the greater good • Their passion for the cause is all-encompassing • They are pragmatic, flexible and generous if they can relate it to their cause.	• Driven by challenge as seek constant stimulation and unsolvable problems to overcome. • Get bored very fast and require variety but will not stop until they have solved it. • Success defined by the size of the challenge or odds overcome • Challenge can be personal (an athlete) or humanitarian (Elon Musk and SpaceX) or organizational (market-share)

Autonomy/ Independence	Security/ Stability	Lifestyle	Technical/ Functional
• Primary need is to work under own rules • Prefer to work alone - setting your own pace, schedule, lifestyle and work habits • Avoid standards as see organisational life as too restrictive, irrational and/or intrusive. • Require flexibility regarding all aspects of work • May turn down opportunities to retain autonomy.	• Seek stability and continuity as primary factor in life. • Avoid risks and hate change – generally seen as "lifers" • Will do whatever is required of them in order to maintain job security, a decent income, and a stable future. • They will accept their organisation's definition of their career and will trust them to do the right thing by them. • Less concerned about content or seniority than by their stability	• Look at the whole pattern of their life and require it all to be integrated. • Personal/family/work/play/social life – it's all part of the one equation to be balanced. • Driven by a need for independence and autonomy over all of their life. • May work excessively to take long period off or work to rote – 9-5 exactly • Often separate passion from work – just a means to an end so not worth compromising on	• Likes to be good. The Guru. The Expert. • Likes to be challenged, and use their skills to meet it. • Self-image is tied up with feeling of competence. • Only interested in management within their area of expertise. • it is the expertise that really turns them on

1970's is a loooong time ago – is this still relevant?

Yes, the world is very different now to how it was in the 70s/80s when Schein was doing his detailed research. He has acknowledged this and in fact suggested that career development in the 21st century depended not only on one's own interests but also on the massive changes in organisational and political environments of businesses. The combination of organisational uncertainties and new technologies that worked to encourage creativity, focussed interest on business ownership as a career path. Therefore, Schein concluded that career anchors were now as much environmental as personal.

Extending this concept, others found greater variance in the motivation of business owners to both pursue and remain self-employed. The old system of lifetime jobs with predictable career paths and stable pay had been replaced by employment relationships that rely on market-based transactions, temporary staffing, short-term contracts and outsourcing. The only thing an employer guarantees an employee are opportunities, but that's it.

This means that going it alone is a career path which is now an accessible and attractive choice for more types of anchors than ever before, and now depend on many more factors:

> ➤ economic climate,
> ➤ events in one's personal life,
> ➤ intentions - whether lifelong or latent,
> ➤ recognition of an opportunity when the right situation emerges,
> ➤ accumulated experiences gained through working for someone else.

Indeed, Schein's research has recognised this change and reconfirmed it's validity – so we're all good to continue to use it. Yay!

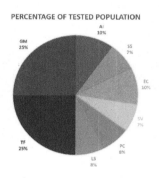

PERCENTAGE OF TESTED POPULATION

For most of the 1970's and 1980's the researchers obtained fairly consistent results with roughly 25% anchored in 'general management', and 'technical/functional'; 10% each in 'autonomy' and 'security' and the rest spread across the remaining anchors. This distribution was valid in every occupation, even though one might imagine that some occupations would be highly biased toward a given anchor.

Since then we have seen an increase in the Lifestyle, Pure Challenge, Service or Dedication and Entrepreneurial Creativity anchors. General Management remains the strongest anchor, and Technical/Functional has seen the most decline (perhaps impacted by the speed of technological advances and accessibility). Furthermore, those with the Security anchor are feeling the most pressure in today's ways of working.

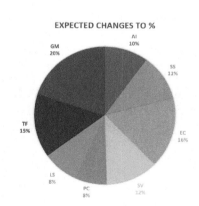

EXPECTED CHANGES TO %

Evidently the main effect is that people are having to become more self-reliant, and are looking more and more inside of themselves to find fulfilment in their career – be that financially, ways of working or the impact they can make. Therefore, the ability to analyse oneself, as well as the ability to figure out what kind of career/job is available, and how their particular anchor best fits into that is the key challenge.

READY TO KNOW WHAT YOURS IS?

Career anchors can be measured by qualitative or quantitative methodologies. As this is a self-study book, we're opting for the quantitative way. Which is to use Schein's 'Career Orientation Inventory'. This consists of 40 statements, five for each of the eight career anchors and a rating scale of 1-6 detailing the degree to which you feel that statement is true for you. These scores are then averaged in order to give you your dominant anchor.

We are clearly a balance of them all, but here we're looking for the strongest score as this is going to contain your 'must-have' or walk-away or deal-breakers, that we are going to need to include in your consideration of business ownership.

As I said, all the anchors can make successful business owners, but there are definitely some that are better suited. I don't want to influence how you answer the questions, so test first and discussion after (I'm trusting you with this...).

For ease, I've automated the scoring etc, so all you need to do is download the excel spreadsheet, complete it and then come back to this point.

The exercise is available from the iaay website–you need to download the exercises: iaay.uk/resources

Let's do This Exercise

WHAT DID YOURS TELL YOU?

OK, so when you've completed your personal profile you'll have a table that looks something like this (this is my actual profile) which shows that my dominant Career Anchor is Service, with a very strong Pure Challenge second and Technical/Functional third...

TF		GM		AU		SE		EC		SV		CH		LS	
1	5	2	4	3	4	4	3	5	1	6	4	7	4	8	1
9	4	10	4	11	4	12	1	13	2	14	5	15	5	16	3
17	3	18	1	19	1	20	2	21	3	22	4	23	4	24	2
25	1	26	2	27	3	28	2	29	2	30	9	31	9	32	1
33	9	34	2	35	2	36	2	37	2	38	4	39	3	40	1
TOTAL	22		13		14		10		10		26		25		8
Ave.	4.4		2.6		2.8		2		2		5.2		5		1.6

As mentioned, every anchor type can be a successful business owner – some just need to be tailored more to ensure success.

What were you? Does it resonate? So let's look at the challenges and benefits of each type:

Benefits:

- ✓ The business is yours, so you can set it up to your rules and models
- ✓ Self-reliance is a key strength as starting a business mean the buck stops with you on all matters
- ✓ Often driven to thinking about running their own business as a means of enabling a better work/life balance - will be better at drawing the boundaries and sticking to them
- ✓ could potentially move faster as you're very clear on how and why you are doing things

Challenges:

- Regardless of company or focus, you will always have to work with other people. You are not an Island.
- An unwillingness to delegate will increase the pressure and remit of your work - this will increase stress and can extend the timescales by when work can be completed, as by one is slower than shared
- Being a business owner often means having to be humble and accept that your way is not the only or best way. Letting go and listening to advice may be harder if you are an AU Anchor
- If you do recognise the need for support or expertise, you can be quite aloof and dismissive - making it harder to work together effectively

Benefits:

- ✓ Everyone has a need for some sense of security, this may result in a more cautious business plan, which will be more structured, safe and workable
- ✓ Being able to structure and tailor business to what makes you feel secure could mean you're clearer on your vision and goals, which will make it easier to make decisions that will bring them to reality
- ✓ If your second strongest anchor is TF, then you may be able to gain sufficient confidence in your expertise to offset the anxiety

Challenges:

- Starting a business has no guarantees - which will increase anxiety in SE Anchors, which could make you nervous of making the big decisions
- Tend to like to follow instructions to obtain guaranteed results - but when you are in charge there are no instructions and no guarantees
- Tend to prefer to remain within comfort zone, so dealing with the daily failure and challenges of getting a business going could induce high levels of stress
- The need to have total faith in yourself and be self-reliant is hard when SE Anchors are accustomed to an external locus of security

Benefits:

- ✓ Incorporating your working life into your personal life is inherently part of being a business owner, so that will appeal to LS Anchors
- ✓ This is a common anchor type for partner businesses - working with your partner can be great
- ✓ A 'lifestyle' business is a common driver for many people considering business ownership - they want a business that means they can travel, work part-time

Challenges:

- The integration may be hard for family members - where does work end?
- A lack of boundaries can cause stress - working all the time can lead to unrealistic expectations
- If personal or family demand are high, then finding the space and time that a new business requires could be challenging
- Starting a business as a LS Anchor could create additional decisions that need to be made if the needs of the business encroaches on the wider family/personal aspect.

Benefits:

✓ The ability to share expertise with the world is a great asset and a good reason to start a business, especially if you accept the need for support in other areas and push yourself to broaden your knowledge

✓ The quality of the content of the business will be exceptional and in-line with your metric of competence

✓ Self-confidence and self-reliance are key traits, so having faith in your own knowledge stands TF Anchors in good stead

✓ TFs enjoy a challenge and the opportunity to learn more and extending an expertise means you can become very competent at the wider business areas needed to be a successful business owner

Challenges:

• Being a business owner is a broad role, which requires the ability to address many different aspects that will challenge the TF Anchor's need to lead from competence

• Wishing to remain in your expertise comfort zone may result in an imbalance in the work progressed and the maturity of the business, which could impact on success and validity

• Considering yourself as the expert may make you closed-minded to how best to tackle the business-side of the business

Benefits:

✓ GM's expertise in analysis, people management and dealing with challenges are all very well suited to business ownership

✓ Your practical skillset, which ensuring balancing many needs and keeping progress moving means, along with strong decision-making will stand them in good stead

✓ GM's thrive on taking responsibility and that is a great asset for a business owner

✓ Some GM's are great at systems and businesses need systems - that work 24/7 even when the business owner isn't.

Challenges:

• Successful business owners have a deep passion for what they are doing. GM's may struggle with making that connection at the start of their business journey - making the business effective but not necessary engaging

• At the start there may be no-one to manage – beyond themselves, and that may be challenging to a GM Anchor where the interpersonal and the scale is part of their metric of success.

• They may over-extend themselves too quickly - hiring people and putting in place lots of processes before the business is ready just to have things to manage

• May be too focussed on the engineering aspects of the business, and miss the big picture aspects

Benefits:

✓ Passion will be evident

✓ Willingness to take calculated risks to get started/ahead

✓ Creativity often means that the businesses you start are market-changers and if you have a strong SV anchor too then humanity is in for a pleasant surprise

✓ If combined with an LS Anchor, then we're looking smaller scale and changing a very niche issue

✓ Combined with the TF anchor and you've got a technical expertise and guru status that will be well articulated

Challenges:

• Can get bored by the mundane admin side of running a business

• Big picture versus detail can be imbalanced

• Not an island - can be closed-minded and not accept alternative views

• Wealth as a success metric can lead to frustration, and starting a business can be a variable process with ups and downs and wealth does not result quickly

Benefits:

✓   We can all name businesses that link to causes - if you have an SV Anchor that passion will go a long way, as long as you can be realistic on how it serves you too

✓   If you have a TF anchor too and they align then that's a strong combination for starting a cause-based business

✓   A strong EC anchor here could make your business aspirations massive and ensure you possess the constitution to take the calculated risks to really affect change

✓   There are many ways that a business can serve a cause - giving, sponsorship etc. as well as direct impact, so think laterally on how to achieve this anchor

Challenges:

- Passion doesn't always translate to effective process. An SC Anchor can sometimes be so tied to the specific outcome that they are blind to the various routes to the same end
- Combined with strength in the TF Anchor could be conflict of interests that challenges the business journey
- Combined with EC can cause issues as Wealth and Service can be opposing metrics at the start of the journey - if you put wealth first then service can be tied directly into the growth

Benefits:

✓   Will take on challenges or problems that successfully solved will make a big difference to clients/society

✓   Won't be phased by the inevitable challenges/failures and pitfalls along the way - will only make the PC Anchor more determined

✓   Combined with a strong SV anchor or EC Anchor and you've got a veritable feast of inherent business ownership strengths

✓   Combined with TF and you're on track to an 'expert in...' business model

Challenges:

- Unsolvable problems take a lot of work...
- You sometimes don't take the obvious route that will work, because it's too easy
- Can over-complicate the product/service, the business model or the message in ways that add extra challenge
- Would need to ensure that had someone involved to act as a reality-check

SUMMARY:

No matter what behavioural profile or dominant anchor you have, you can be a successful business owner. It's about empowering yourself through self-knowledge to have a deep and honest understanding of yourself, so that you can consciously make choices and decisions that best serve you and your business.

USING INTEGRAL THEORY

Making the decision to set up a business is a big one. It changes everything. So it needs to be a considered, thought-through and consciously made choice.

Having completed the initial section and considered your career anchors and behavioural profile, the rest of the book uses the basic concepts of Ken Wilbur's integral theory to look at the proposition from four different perspectives to ensure you are able to make your decisions in that way.

WHAT IS INTEGRAL THEORY AND WHY IS IT USEFUL HERE

Integral theory is Ken Wilber's attempt to place a wide diversity of theories into one single, simple framework. It is portrayed as a 'theory of everything' ("the living Totality of matter, body, mind, soul, and spirit").

Ken Wilber's AQAL ('All Quadrants All Levels')[6], pronounced "ah-qwul", is the basic framework of integral theory, and the only part that we will be using. It suggests that all human knowledge and experience can be placed in a four-quadrant grid, along the axes of 'interior-exterior' and 'individual-collective'. It synthesizes eastern traditions with western structure to create a model that describes human development simplistically and holistically.

My intent in using this model is to shift your awareness away from any limitations you might sense, towards your highest possible future. In order to overcome our current concerns, we must find new ways of thinking. We must expand our point of view and our perspective. So whilst this may seem, at first viewing, to be overly intellectual, at its core it is actually incredibly simple to understand and apply.

Every event in the world has three dimensions from which it can be viewed and assessed from – I, we, and it. You can look at any event from the point of view of the 'I' (or how I personally see or feel about the event) from the point of view of the 'we' (how not just I but others see the event) and as an 'it' (objective facts of the event.)

If you leave out any of those dimensions, something is going to be missing, something will get 'broken'. All three perspectives are necessary to be fully informed. So fundamental are these dimensions of 'I', 'we' and 'it' that they form the basis of integral theory, called the four quadrants, (four quadrants come from dividing 'it' into singular and plural).

Thus, an integrally informed path will take all of these dimensions into account, and arrive at a more comprehensive and effective outcome.

The four quadrants are fairly simple to understand, they are the inside and the outside of the individual and the collective. Together the entire human experience can be categorised and analysed, which is what we want to use this for.

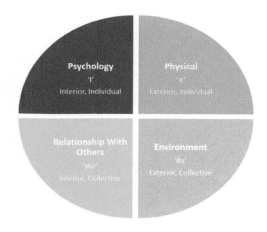

Wilber uses this grid to categorise the perspectives of various theories and scholars, for example:

- **Interior individual – 'I' – Psychology (upper-left quadrant)** is all about the self and our own consciousness – what our perspective is, what matters to me, my thoughts, feelings, values, meanings, intentions. It's about things like cognitive awareness, emotional access and interpersonal skills.
- **Interior plural – 'We' – Relationship with Others (lower-left)** seeks to interpret the collective consciousness of a society, the culture, conversations and conventions we mutually understand and use to relate to each other. Here it's about worldview and cultural values.
- **Exterior individual – 'It' – Physical (upper-right)** limits itself to the observation of the behaviour of organisms that can be visibly seen and measured. What people can see about you, your brainwaves, neural systems, nutritional intake, hormonal and immune responses.
- **Exterior plural – 'Its' Environment (lower-right)** focuses upon the behaviour of society – design, process, structures and systems of procedures that support, explain, map, measure and guide how things work.

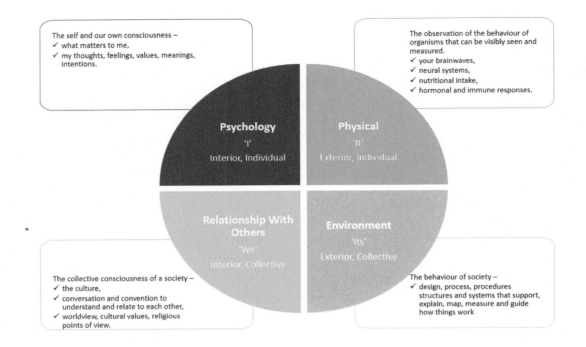

The self and our own consciousness –
- ✓ what matters to me,
- ✓ my thoughts, feelings, values, meanings, intentions.

The observation of the behaviour of organisms that can be visibly seen and measured.
- ✓ your brainwaves,
- ✓ neural systems,
- ✓ nutritional intake,
- ✓ hormonal and immune responses.

Psychology
'I'
Interior, Individual

Physical
'It'
Exterior, Individual

Relationship With Others
'We'
Interior, Collective

Environment
'Its'
Exterior, Collective

The collective consciousness of a society –
- ✓ the culture,
- ✓ conversation and convention to understand and relate to each other,
- ✓ worldview, cultural values, religious points of view.

The behaviour of society –
- ✓ design, process, procedures structures and systems that support, explain, map, measure and guide how things work

According to Wilber, all four quadrants offer complementary, rather than contradictory, perspectives. It is possible for all to be correct, and all are necessary for a complete account of human existence; each by itself offers only a partial view of reality.

Modern western society has a pathological focus on the exterior or objective perspective. Such perspectives tend to value that which can be externally measured and tested in a laboratory but tend to deny or marginalise the left sides (subjectivity, individual experience, feelings, values) as *unproven* or having *no meaning*.

Knowing all four quadrants allows you to see where problems might arise by bringing awareness to it. It allows you to simplify any complex problem by breaking it down to real issues – and this identifies the blocked quadrant.

What integral theory shows is that a block in just one of the quadrants will negatively impact the likelihood and effectiveness of whatever you want coming to fruition. All of the quadrants interlink and impact each other, therefore the quadrant you don't look at will contain the challenges that stop you from succeeding.

Let's take an example….

You want to lose weight. So you buy a programme that teaches you a specific diet mentality – i.e. how you think and feel, so that is a Psychology quadrant approach. Tick!

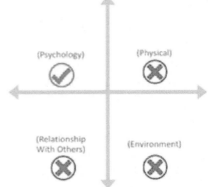

But what if your family situation means you're surrounded by the bad foods you need to avoid. That's an environmental block.

Looking at the physical, you're having cravings for the sugar you're missing – that's a block.

And you are concerned about how others will think of you if you fail – oops that's a Relationship with others issue.

So oh dear this approach only addresses one quadrant. How likely are you to be successful in this instance? It's simply not sustainable – like a chair with a broken leg or a car with flat tyres.

In order for change to be long-lasting you must align all four quadrants

You can use this theory to assist you with any challenge in life. Firstly, take the problematic issue or event and list everything that is needed to achieve that goal. Then assign each item on the list to it's appropriate quadrant, based on the interior/exterior, individual/collective perspective. I do this diagrammatically. You can then see where the imbalances are and create a plan to address and re-balance things. To help, there's a template available on the Exercise page of the website or by clicking the link below….

The exercise is available from the iaay website–you need to download the exercises: iaay.uk/resources

<u>Go To Your Integral Theory Template</u>

HOW WE ARE GOING TO USE INTEGRAL THEORY

I have asked the question, "What is needed to make the decision to be a business owner?" and I've brainstormed on the key aspects within each of the four quadrants, as outlined above. I placed them on the quadrant diagram and then prioritised the top three in each area, and this will be the structure for the remainder of the book.

We will work through each quadrant, exploring how that quadrant's perspective is relevant and doing exercises to assist us in creating our comprehensive and integrated answer to the question. I may also make recommendations for further insight if you desire it, such as useful books, articles, videos etc…. I do this because I don't want to slow the process by spending too much time getting into the detail, but I think you may like some of them enough to want to know more.

Value Hierarchy Limiting Beliefs Financial Beliefs		Impacts of Stress Resilience Mind Body Relationship	
Psychology	**I**	**It**	**Physical**
Relationship With Others	**We**	**Its**	**Environment**
Family Support Network Partnerships		Current work Financial Setup Cultural Expectations	

Ready? Good! Let's get started with Quadrant 1: Psychology (I)

QUADRANT 1 – PSYCHOLOGY/ 'I'

In this section we are going to explore your psychology – your sense of self and how this relates to your desire and preparedness to be a business owner.

In the integral theory diagram I outlined three main areas we will cover:

1. **Values**
2. **Financial Mindset**
3. **Limiting Beliefs**

1. YOUR VALUE HIERARCHY

So let's get started with getting to know yourself. Here we utilise the method and models of human behavioural psychology as espoused by Dr. John Demartini and others for the purpose of insight and challenge in a way that is constructive and relevant.

'If you take responsibility for your life and ask quality questions about how to fulfil it, you become a magnet for opportunities. People and money are irresistibly drawn to energy, enthusiasm, and certainty.' - Dr. John Demartini [7]

WHAT ARE VALUES?

For a lot of people, this term conjures up a variety of things including abstract qualities such as honesty, integrity or trust. Or a set of religious beliefs, a patriotic ideal or a code of morality. These are not what we mean when we refer to personal values. In this context, personal values are the true driving force that shape perceptions, decisions, actions and feelings.

Values are as specific to you as your fingerprints, your retinal pattern, and your voiceprint. Perhaps what is truly valued most is spending time with family, listening to a beautiful piece of music, or having the chance to play football several times a week. Our highest values are known to change throughout our lifetime but they are still the very essence of who we are, what we're drawn to, what we inevitably seek out, and what we live for.

Values are like an internal compass, pointing us towards the activities, people and places that most fulfil us. They lead us away from the situations and people that are most likely to feel unfulfilling.

"Just like no one else can choose your fingerprints, or alter the pattern of your retina, no outside authority – no parent, teacher, political leader or religious figure – can define your values. Only you can look into your own mind, heart and soul and discover what is truly most important to you."

- Dr. John Demartini

WHY ARE VALUES POWERFUL?

"Your unique purpose is to understand and fulfil your highest values.
It is both a spiritual quest, and the key to a fulfilling life."
- Dr. John Demartini

For an individual seeking purpose in life, values are powerful in helping them discover who they are, what they want to do with their life and the direction they can take in order to fulfil this.

For a business owner, an understanding of values and the role they play are powerful in four ways:

1) An acknowledgement of what matters to you will give you insight into the type of business owner you will be, what you want the business to deliver for you in terms of intellectual challenge, lifestyle enhancements, societal change (relating back to your anchors).
2) It will help you appreciate and be honest about what is of value to you – this may provide inspiration or awareness of where your business idea came from or why you're passionate about it.
3) It will also tell you where your challenges may lie – if your business idea is not related to your higher values that's going to prove difficult.
4) In a wider context, knowing your current values is so useful as it helps explain changes in relationships, views, desires etc.

"Your highest values determine your attention, retention and intention:
what you notice, what you remember, what you intend or act upon"
- Dr. John Demartini

WHAT ARE YOUR HIGHEST VALUES?

Clarity regarding your personal values (your sub-conscious list of priorities) helps define your personal WHY YOU DO WHAT YOU DO, which will lend itself to helping you more clearly articulate the type of business owner will be.

So now that we can see how fundamental it is to understand our personal values, it's time to discover them.

===============

The following exercise uses an adaption of Dr. Demartini's 13-step 'Value Determination Exercise' [8]. We do this because it's simple, quick to do, but massively effective and illuminating. It is based on the universal laws of energy, the insight of many philosophers, psychologists, doctors and practitioners the world over. It has proven over and over to provide actionable insight.

STEP ONE:

Answer the following ten questions, with three examples for each. For each question, choose the three examples that are most important to you. Please note that long sentences explaining yourself are not necessary, this is just for you.

1. How do you fill your personal space?

Look around your home or office, do you see family photos, sports trophies, business awards, books? Do you see beautiful objects, comfortable furniture for friends to sit on, or souvenirs of favourite places you've visited? Perhaps your space is full of games, puzzles, DVDs, CDs, or other forms of entertainment? Do you have books, files and notebooks full of study material? Do you have books and products relating to health enhancement? When you look in your bag, what items do you consistently carry with you as you don't like to leave the house without them?

Whatever you see around you is a very strong clue as to what you value most. So what three things in your space represent you most?

2. How do you spend your time?

You make time for things that are really important to you, and run out of time for things that aren't. Even though people usually say, "I don't have time for what I really want to do", the truth is that they are too busy doing what is truly important to them. You find time for things that are really important to you; somehow, you figure it out. So how do you spend your time? Which three actions do you spend your time on most?

I.e. Checking out the gossip on Facebook (you can put it down as passive socialising if you want); playing games on your phone; listening to music; studying; going to the gym; travelling; watching films; shopping.

3. How do you spend your energy?

You have energy for the things that inspire you – the things you value most – whilst you run out of energy for things that do not inspire you. That's because things that are low among your values drain you, whereas things that are high among your values energise you. In fact, when you are doing something that you value highly, you have more energy afterwards than when you started because you're doing something that you love and are inspired by. Maybe you love to play football so much that you feel energised after the game even if you're tired. So which three activities do you get your energy from?

I.e. Playing cards with your mates right into the early morning; making that big sale come through on the job; working on your motorbike; cycling around Hyde Park; attending a workshop to learn about fitness; planning your holidays

4. How do you spend your money?

Again, you find money for things that are valuable to you, but you don't want to part with money for things that are not important to you. So your choices about spending money tell you a great deal about what you value most. These can be experiences, objects, and services, anything really. What are the three items you spend most of your money on and always find money for?

I.e. Hiring a cleaner because you don't get dirty to be clean; the best headphones because you're an audiophile; sky-diving through the Swiss Alps. Come on, do you really need examples for this one?

At this point you may be noticing some overlaps and similarities between your answers – this is a great sign. It means that you have already aligned a lot of your highest values, goals and daily activities. If you notice a lot of divergence between the answers to these first four questions, you might not be being totally honest – maybe you are deferring to a social idealism of what you 'should' do, so please ensure you're being totally honest as you'll then get the most out of this exercise.

5. Where do you have the most order and organisation?

We bring order and organisation to things that are important to us, and allow chaos and disorder to rein in relation to things that are low on our values. It could be your social calendar, your dietary regimen, your clothes and wardrobe, your business, your finances, your spiritual rituals, your cooking area, or your house. Everyone has some item or area of life that is most organised. Which three items or areas do you have most organisation in?

6. Where are you most reliable, disciplined and focused?

You don't have to be prodded from the outside to do things that you value the most; you are inspired from within to do these things and so you do them. Look at the activities, relationships, and goals for which you are disciplined, reliable and focused – the things that nobody has to get at you to do. Which three activities are you most reliable or disciplined at doing?

7. What are your internal dialogue topics?

What do you keep talking to yourself about the most? Not negative self-talk. What you think to yourself about what you desire – internal dialogues that actually seem to be coming true. Which three outcomes about how you would love your life to be do you talk to yourself about most?

For example, your internal dialogue about that dream holiday – that you're researching for, or the relationship that you know you are going to have one day. Or that by the end of the year you will be debt-free.

8. What do you talk about in social settings?

Now here's a clue that you'll probably notice for other people as well as yourself. What are the topics that you keep wanting to bring into conversations that nobody has to remind you to talk about? What subjects turn you into an instant extravert? Topics that immediately bring you to life and start you talking. You can use the same insight to analyse other people's values. If someone asks you about your kids, that means that either their kids or your kids are important to them. If they say, "How's business?" they value business. If they ask, "Are you seeing anyone new?" then relationships matter to them. Topics that attract you are a key indicator of what you value. Which three topics do you keep wanting to talk to others about most?

9. What inspires you?

What inspires you? Who inspires you? What is common to the people that inspire you? Figuring out what inspires you most reveals what you value most. Which three people, actions or outcomes inspire you most, and what is common to them?

10. What are the most consistent long-term goals you have set?

What are the three long-term goals, that you have been focussing on, that you are bringing into reality? Again, we're not talking about fantasies here. We want the dreams you are bringing into reality, slowly but surely, the dreams that have been dominating your mind and your thoughts for a while. So which are the three most important goals that you keep focussing on, that are gradually coming true and you have evidence of happening.

I.e. To be financially comfortable enough to work part-time; to design and market technology that will be bigger than the iPhone; to write a book; to become a public speaker; to own a range of properties; to climb to Everest Base Camp now and at the age of 65 (unless your 65 now, then this is awkward).

STEP TWO:

Now that you have three answers to each of the 10 questions, it's time to identify the answers that repeat most often.

You'll have noticed that among your 30 answers there is a certain amount of repetition (maybe even a lot of repetition). You are expressing the same kinds of values in different ways – for example, *"Spending time with people I like", "having a drink with my work colleagues", "Going out to eat with my friends"* – if you look closely you'll see patterns beginning to emerge.

Look at your answers and assess the answer that is most often repeated, and write beside it the number of times it occurs. Then find the second most frequent answer, then the third, and so on, until you have ranked every single answer. This gives you a good primary indicator of what your highest values are, and the hierarchy of them.

For example, if 'looking after my health' turned up 9 times, and 'spending time with family' turned up 8 times, and 'fitness' turned up 6 times, you would see that your highest value is….

STEP THREE:

Based on how often your answers appear and repeat, create a list of your five most important values in priority order, with the most important first…

This list gives you your hierarchy of values – a structure that you can start to build your life around and make decisions from. Did you see similarities coming through with the previous exercises? Did you gain an insight into yourself that resonated? I know that we all talk about the things we want to do but that we don't quite find the time to do. When you understand your values it becomes clear – it's not that we don't find the time, it's quite simply that they are just not aligned to your highest values…

=============

So if we now have a clear view of your current, natural behavioural profile, our dominant career anchor and our value hierarchy, then surely we're in great stead to understand ourselves within the context of the 'I' quadrant….

Yes, and no… there are two other key areas that I want you to explore within this quadrant – these are imperative to accept and reflect upon because they are the self-limiting beliefs and repressed emotions that can cause blocks in this quadrant, and we want to become conscious of them so we can eliminate them!

As a business owner, the primary one I want to address is your financial mindset.

2. YOUR FINANCIAL MIND-SET

Running a business requires money – there's no two ways about that, and understanding your mindset about money as a business owner is key. I am aiming to help you understand how money fits into your values, enabling you to be mindful of what you want versus what you need, and to ensuring you are aligned personally, in order to bring financial success professionally.

WHY TALK ABOUT MONEY?

Money is the fuel that drives business.

Unfortunately, many businesses that fail cite financial issues – especially cash flow challenges - as one of the main causes, whether that failure be in their first year, or five years down the line.

The challenge with money is that it doesn't always flow. It can be seen as a major barrier in being able to manifest the business of your vision. It costs money to set things up, it costs money to have a team, and you have to spend money before you get it back in revenue. These are all challenges that business owners know only too well. Added to this is the level of accountability and responsibility that you feel to those you have hired and to your friends and family that have supported you in bringing your business vision into reality. Guilt and shame often mean that a business owner will go without to ensure the business keeps moving forward.

The statistics on the failure rate of small companies are scary, and having worked so hard you don't want your financial management to prevent you from manifesting your business dreams.

WHAT WE ARE NOT GOING TO TALK ABOUT

To be clear, we are not going to talk about how to best structure your business, how to price your products or services, your supply chain management, your payment terms, or how to manage your tax affairs – there are lots of far better places to go to get that kind of advice.

WHAT WE ARE GOING TO TALK ABOUT

What we are talking about here is the role that money plays in underpinning your business from a 'you' perspective. Your attitude to money and its role in the achievement of your vision, and therefore your management of it, is as important as the detailed day-to-day focus on cash flow.

MONEY IS JUST A FORM OF EXCHANGE

Money is a means or medium of exchange. It has no moral value, it is neither good nor bad, right nor wrong, positive nor negative. It's merely an exchange of one person's value for another.

Today, money has evolved to be a commodity in its own right, and many people have a high value on financial security or independence, or lifestyle aspects that require a certain level of wealth. At its core, money **cannot and must not be** the reason-to-be for a business, it is purely an input and an output that represent the exchange you are putting into the manifestation of your vision.

Every human has two innate driving forces; a spiritual force which is all about the quest for a degree of immortality (in a business sense read that as a legacy – creating something that exists after you've gone). Secondly a material force which is driving for financial freedom (all the options that come from what money can buy you – both in business and in your personal life).

For many people these forces are not balanced, the material force takes control which results in a narcissistic attitude to money that is all about what they get, not what they can give. It is not a fair exchange, which is always necessary if it's to be sustained.

The Egyptians had a saying:

"Spiritual drive without the material -is expressionless. Material drive without the spiritual is motionless. Only when they are intertwined do you get a driving force that is both immortal and freeing."

This is the reason that most get-rich-quick schemes are actually get-poor-quick schemes as they are not balanced between these driving forces. From an energy perspective, this means that you expect to receive more than you give, and in order to reach balance again you therefore have to lose more than you get. This results in a stagnation in terms of direction, delivery and execution.

Wealth means well-being – the ability to do what you love and love what you do. As Dr Demartini says, 'To be wealthy is to live in a world where your vocation and vacation become synonymous'. It's the achievement of self-actualisation. This is the aspect that comes from the spiritual driving force.

So in order to have effective money management in your business and to build yourself the financial rewards that you desire, you have to ensure that how you perceive wealth is a fair and equitable exchange.

The human psyche makes this hard – we have internal unconscious motives, created by society, family, experience and other external values that mean we internally sabotage our wealth building capabilities. We are told that to be 'good' or 'blessed' we must give more than we receive. This is just not true. History shows that:

"Cultures that did not develop fair exchange or learn how to manage their money stagnated and did not develop to make any real contribution to the world (be that in the realms of art, science, religion, or philosophy). Only cultures that learn the art and mastery of wealth building and fair exchange management of economics have contributed, expanded and prospered".

- Dr. John Demartini

The same is true for individuals, and therefore for you, as a business owner.

In this section, we are going to explore five basic principles of wealth building and fair exchange management so that you too can reap the rewards of what you are giving to the world through the manifestation of your business.

PRINCIPLE ONE: YOU MUST APPRECIATE MONEY FOR IT TO GROW

Money offers great opportunities – it enables you to build a business that can reach hundreds of thousands of people and effect positive change. It can enable you to innovate, break old rules, and create new ones. It can fund philanthropic ventures; it keeps a roof over your head.

A key principle is that you must appreciate money if you want it to grow. If you manage it wisely, then you will be given more to manage.

Your attitude to money is dictated by your value hierarchy (as we've explored). This value hierarchy dictates how you spend your money – or rather on what you spend your money. For instance, someone with a high value on health will spend more than the average person on quality food, health supplements and anything that they perceive as benefitting their health. Another person may see this person's bank account detailing their spending and be shocked at what they perceive as extravagant spending, because their values will result in them spending their money differently.

Values are derived predominantly from what you perceive is missing in your life – a void if you like. Voids drive values. So if financial security or independence are not in your top three to five values then, to quote Dr Demartini, you will find that you probably have "… less money at the end of your month, than month at the end of your money".

At a very simplistic level, it is not how much money you make that counts but rather the hierarchy of values which dictate how you manage and spend it, that does. If your lifestyle is more important that financial security or independence, then you will raise it as soon as your wealth increases. If immediate gratification is a stronger value (i.e. the material driving force) then being a business owner is probably not the right path for you.

To be successful in business you need to be able to pass-up immediate gratification for long-term vision, this will result in you accumulating enough money so that eventually it is working for you, rather than you working for it.

Those who appreciate money tend to put their money where it appreciates in value. Those that don't appreciate money tend to spend it on things that depreciate in value. This is just nature's way of reflecting your perceptions of money and their value hierarchy.

> *"To those who have, more is given, to those that haven't, more is taken away."*
>
> - **Proverb**

The best place to start the transformation of your financial destiny is to complete the following exercise that focusses on your financial past.

===============

EXERCISE - PAST MONIES [9]

The subject of money can be a tricky one for many people, especially when they don't perceive that they have enough, so this is a really simple exercise to assist you.

No matter what your current financial situation is, the very thought that you don't have enough money is enough to ensure you continue not having enough money. It is a reflection of being ungrateful for the money you do and have had.

When you have little money it can feel challenging to feel grateful, but when you understand that nothing will change until you're grateful for it, and that it's easy to get into a place of gratitude, you will be inspired to do it.

It's important that you read through the entire exercise before starting, and ideally Step 1 of this exercise is done first thing in the morning, so you have all day to complete Step 2.

STEP 1:

Sit down and take a few minutes to think back through your childhood, before you had any or much money. As you recall each memory where money was paid for you, say and feel the words, "thank you", with all your heart in each instance:

➢ *Did you always have food to eat?*
➢ *Did you live in a home?*
➢ *Did you receive an education over many years?*
➢ *How did you travel to school each day?*

- ➤ *Did you have schoolbooks, school lunches, and all the things you needed for school?*
- ➤ *Did you go on any holidays when you were a child?*
- ➤ *What were the most exciting birthday gifts you received when you were a child?*
- ➤ *Did you have a bike, toys, a pet?*
- ➤ *Did you have clothes, as you grew so quickly from one size to another?*
- ➤ *Did you ever go to the cinema, play sports, learn a musical instrument, or have a hobby?*
- ➤ *Did you go to the doctor and take medicine when you were not well?*
- ➤ *Did you go to the dentist?*
- ➤ *Did you have the essential items that you used every day, like your toothbrush, toothpaste, soap and shampoo?*
- ➤ *Did you travel in a car?*
- ➤ *Did you watch television, make phone calls, use lights, electricity, and water?*

All of these things cost money, and you received them all – at no charge! As you travel back through memories of your childhood and youth, you'll realise how many things you received that equate to hard-earned cash. Be grateful for every single instance and memory.

STEP 2:

Now find a small note (£5/ $1/ EU5) and take a post-it note or sticker and on that sticker write:

"THANK YOU FOR ALL THE MONEY I'VE BEEN GIVEN THROUGHOUT MY LIFE".

Stick this on the note.

Take this magic fiver with you today, and put it in your wallet or purse or pocket. At least twice during the course of the day, take it out, hold it and read your written words and be truly grateful for the abundance of money you've been given in your life. The sincerer you are, and the more you feel it, the better.

After today, put the magic fiver in a place you will continue to see it every day to remind you to be grateful. I have mine in my wallet – it looks pretty beaten up, but it means that every time I go to pay for something that requires a card or cash, I see it and think about what I'm spending money on….

===============

PRINCIPLE TWO: STOP CARRYING GUILT THAT MAKES YOU FEEL UNWORTHY

As explained earlier, the society we grow up in shapes us, and creates internal unconscious motives that sabotage our wealth building capabilities, based on a perception of what is right and wrong. This creates guilt and shame that we carry around with us, that prevent us from having a fair exchange that will result in a business enterprise succeeding to its optimal potential.

From a psychological perspective, the diagram below explains how guilt and shame are created and the effects it can have.

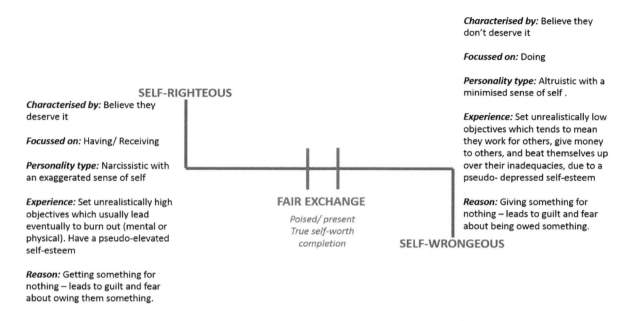

SELF-RIGHTEOUS

Characterised by: Believe they deserve it

Focussed on: Having/ Receiving

Personality type: Narcissistic with an exaggerated sense of self

Experience: Set unrealistically high objectives which usually lead eventually to burn out (mental or physical). Have a pseudo-elevated self-esteem

Reason: Getting something for nothing – leads to guilt and fear about owing them something.

FAIR EXCHANGE

Poised/ present
True self-worth
completion

Characterised by: Believe they don't deserve it

Focussed on: Doing

Personality type: Altruistic with a minimised sense of self .

Experience: Set unrealistically low objectives which tends to mean they work for others, give money to others, and beat themselves up over their inadequacies, due to a pseudo- depressed self-esteem

Reason: Giving something for nothing – leads to guilt and fear about being owed something.

SELF-WRONGEOUS

Whether it's self-righteous or self-wrongous, the resultant emotions of guilt and shame will dramatically affect your ability to manage money.

> *"…until you can manage emotions, don't expect to ever manage money"*
>
> - ***Warren Buffet***

As the diagram shows, the emotions of fear (a future imagined emotion) and guilt (a past remembered emotion) cost you money, because they keep you out of fair exchange and being consciously present. As a result of the emotion, you either exaggerate (self-righteous) or minimise (self-wrongous) your self-worth, which will lead you to setting unrealistic goals – the ability to do things quicker or bigger than you can or conversely that you can't do it at all. Both of these extremes prevent you from being in fair exchange and moving forward.

In all probability you have a list in your mind of things that you've screwed up on and you're holding on to this list in your life. This list, that is causing you to feel guilty about the past or which causes you to project fearfully into the future, is holding you back – so let's do a short exercise now to release that.

===============

EXERCISE: GUILT RELEASER

This may not start out as the easiest of exercises, but having completed the previous ones, you know that the effort will be worth it. So please persist and trust the process.

We all have a list of things that we believe we've screwed up, the things about our past business dealings that we beat ourselves up about. Here are some examples:

➢ *The client we lost*
➢ *The job interview we flunked*
➢ *The job you lost*
➢ *The course you forgot to attend*
➢ *The job you turned down which you later wished you'd taken*
➢ *The report that was late*
➢ *The data that was wrong*
➢ *The risk you took that didn't pay off*
➢ *The bad hire you made*
➢ *The investment that went bad*

They can be big or they can be small. It's not what happened that's important, it's how you feel about it... So start by making a list of them either in your Exercise section of this book or your Journal:

STEP TWO:

Scan over your list again and star the one situation/ example that makes you feel the most guilt, the one that still has the ability to make you feel really bad about yourself, that you still beat yourself up over.

Now taking that example, you're now going drill a little deeper using the table in the exercise section, or your journal:

First re-write the situation/ explanation at the top.

Then you need to think about the situation, firstly from your own point of view, and come up with AT LEAST FIVE benefits that the situation has given to you.

Examples could be:

- *Losing my job meant more time with my family*
- *I learned a lot about investments that meant I made good ones later on*
- *I had to develop my skills as a manager to get the best out of my team*
- *I met a new contact that became an important colleague/client/associate/business partner*
- *Well yes, it was annoying, but the situation did mean that I moved location*
- *I moved company, and actually preferred it at the new one*
- *I made a new friend/contact*
- *I took my career in a different direction*

Once you get into it you'll find benefits in all aspects of your life (the seven areas can be classified as spiritual, mental, physical, social, career, financial, family) if you get stuck, ask about how the situation helped in each of these seven areas.

Once you've done that, move onto and identify AT LEAST FIVE benefits that situation gave to others (either those directly or indirectly involved).

Examples could be:

- *Losing her job meant XXXX moved to one that suited her better*
- *The incorrect data meant the process got changed and money was saved*
- *Your friendship with XXX was saved as you didn't work together anymore*
- *Your kids got to see you more*
- *XXX got to show their knowledge which meant your role evolved to a better place*

Again these can be varied and big or small, but the benefits will be there, if you keep looking...

Why at least five? That's how many it will take to dissolve the guilt you feel about the situation. After listing that many you will start to view it differently, and gratitude for the situation will start to emerge. You do not need to stop at five, if you can do more, then please do, as the more the merrier on this exercise. You can of course also re-do this for all the examples you came up with – you don't need guilt in your life or your business so purge it using this really simple technique.

If you struggle with this exercise, that's ok – it's a tough one when you first try it. You could ask someone you trust to assist you.

===============

What is very clear from this exercise is that there are no mistakes. You are just holding a perception that what happened was a mistake or shouldn't have happened. This is baggage – which means that your feelings of self-worth and your willingness to receive good things, are interfered with (even if unconsciously). It stops you from feeling worthy and makes you want to only give as a form of penance; which pushes you away from fair exchange and into the realms of altruism and self-depreciation.

You need to maintain yourself in fair exchange – where you are willing to receive what you ask for. Put simply, high self-worth equates to high net worth.

PRINCIPLE THREE: HARNESS THE UNIVERSAL LAW OF GRATITUDE

"It is only with gratitude that life becomes rich."

- *Dietrich Bonhoeffer*

Gratitude operates through a universal law that governs your whole life. According to the law of attraction, which governs all the energy in our universe, 'like attracts like'. Often referred to in terms such as 'whatever goes around comes around', or, 'you reap what you sow, you get what you give', these sayings all describe a principle of the universe that Sir Isaac Newton discovered:

"Every action always has an opposite and equal reaction."

When you apply the idea of gratitude to Newton's law it quickly becomes apparent why cultivating a sense of gratitude is so important:

"Every action of giving thanks always causes an opposite reaction of receiving. And what you receive will always be equal to the amount of gratitude you've given. This means that the very action of gratitude sets off a reaction of receiving. And the more sincerely and the more deeply grateful you feel, the more you will receive."

– Rhonda Byrne – The Magic

History is laden with famous people who practiced gratitude, and whose achievements put them among the greatest humans who have ever lived:

- Gandhi
- Martin Luther King Jr.
- Shakespeare
- Newton
- Einstein
- Lincoln
- Jung

When it comes to the relationship between gratitude and money, it can be expressed as gratitude is riches and complaint is poverty; it's the golden rule of your whole life, whether relating to your health, business, relationships or money. The more grateful you can be for the money you have, even if that's currently not very much, the more riches you will receive. Conversely, the more you complain about money, the poorer you will become.

The key is to turn the reasons you complain into an act of gratitude, so it has double the power to change your circumstances.

Most people don't even realise that they are complaining. It happens through people's thoughts, as well as their words, and most people aren't always aware of the many thoughts in their head. Any complaining, negative, jealous or worried thoughts or words about money are literally keeping money from you. If you don't have enough money, paying your bills can be one of the most difficult things to do. It can seem like there is a greater stream of bills than there is money to pay for them. But if you complain about your bills then what you are really doing is complaining about money.

When you don't have sufficient funds for your business, the last thing you would normally do is feel grateful for the bills, but that's exactly what you need to do. To have a profitable business you need to be grateful for every single thing to do with money, and begrudgingly paying your suppliers, overheads and so on, is not being grateful. Instead you must be grateful for the goods and services you've received from those who billed you. It is such a simple thing to do, but it will have a monumental effect on the money in your business.

Let's now learn a really simple but powerful technique in how to be grateful.

===============

EXERCISE: GRATEFUL BILLS [9]

To be grateful for a bill, think about how much you've benefitted from the service or goods on the bill. If it's a payment for office space be grateful to have the space and being in it. What if the only way you could have the office space was by saving up all the money and paying in cash for it? What if there were no such things as lending institutions or places to rent? Most of us would be living and working on the streets, so be grateful to those who have made this possible.

If you're paying a bill for a utility like gas or electric, think about the heating or cooling you've received, the hot water, and every appliance you're able to use because of the service. If you're paying a phone or internet bill imagine how different life would be if you had to travel to talk to each person individually, or access the information in libraries. All of these remarkable services are at your fingertips, so be grateful for them, and be grateful that the companies trust you by providing their services before you paid for them.

STEP ONE:

So now we're going to make this practical. Take any currently unpaid bills you have, and use gratitude's magical power by writing across them, *"Thank you for the money"* and feel grateful for having the money to pay the bill, whether you have it or not.

If you receive and pay most of your bills online, then when you receive an online notification forward it to yourself as an email and write in the subject line in capital letters *"THANK YOU FOR THE MONEY"*.

STEP TWO:

Now, find 10 bills you paid in the past, and write across the front of each one the magic words.

"Thank you – Paid".

As you write on each paid bill, feel as grateful as you possibly can that you had the money to pay the bill. The more gratitude you can harness for the bills you've paid; the more money will be magnetized to you.

================

From this day forward, I invite you to make it a regular habit that whenever you pay a bill, you briefly think of the service you've received from the bill and write across the face of the bill the grateful words, *"Thank you – Paid"*. If you don't have the money to pay the bill, use gratitude's power and write, *"Thank you for the money"*, and feel as if you're saying thank you because you already have the money to pay the bill.

A few years ago, I was re-starting my business, after a challenging split from a business partner that left me with nothing. Paying my rent, my bills, even keeping my website afloat was a struggle every month. I did this exercise and was amazed at the coincidences that happened to enable me to pay every bill I had – a tax refund appeared, a PPI refund came, a new client turned up that wanted to pay upfront. The key element was that I dug really deep and was truly grateful. This isn't something you can pay lip-service to – it's only you you're doing that disservice to by not giving it a go. I was so delighted by the results that I continue this practice to this day.

PRINCIPLE FOUR: DON'T TAKE THE PAST WITH YOU

Once again we are utilising the universal law of gratitude to help us. When you direct gratitude's power toward any negative situation, a new situation is created, eliminating the old one. In other words, when you get to a place where you feel grateful for money, more than you feel a lack of money, a new situation is created, eliminating the lack of money and replacing it with more money.

All negative emotions about money push money away from you and so reduce the overall amount of money in your business (and the rest of your life), and every time you feel bad about money you reduce it a little more. If you have feelings about money like envy, disappointment, worry or fear, you cannot receive more. The law of attraction proves this.

However difficult it may appear to be, you have to ignore the current situation and any lack of money you may currently be experiencing, and gratitude is the guaranteed way for you to do that. You cannot be grateful for money and disappointed with money at the same time. You can't be thinking grateful thoughts and worried or fearful thoughts at the same time.

If you've completed all the exercises in this section then you've already demonstrated your gratitude for the money you've received in the past and learnt a technique to show gratitude in the present, so now it's time to utilise gratitude for your financial future.

Firstly, you need be clear that money comes in many ways, it travels in many forms to get into your business. You need to be mindful and grateful for each of them. Some examples of the various ways are:

- Receiving an unexpected cheque
- An increase in salary
- A tax refund
- A new client finds you
- A lower interest rate is offered to you
- A contract gets extended with a rate increase
- A referral you weren't expecting
- An unanticipated gift of money
- An item you were going to purchase is now discounted
- A client or colleague picks up the tab for a meal, travel, drink
- There's a money-back offer on a purchase
- Someone gives you something they don't need that you were going to buy

The end result of every one of these circumstances is that you have more money. So whenever a situation arises, ask yourself: does this circumstance mean that I have more money? Because if it does, you need to be grateful.

As always, these principles work best when applied practically, so it's time for another exercise.

==============

EXERCISE - GRATITUDE CHEQUE [10]

In the Exercise Book you will find an image of a blank cheque, and you are going to write out a gratitude cheque to yourself. Fill in the amount of money you want to receive, along with your name and today's date. Choose a specific amount of money for one thing your business really wants/needs, because you will feel more grateful for the money when you know what you're going to spend it on.

Money is a means to what you want, but it is not the end result, so if you just thought about money per-se you wouldn't be able to feel as much gratitude. When you imagine getting things you really want, or doing the things you really want to do, you will feel far more gratitude than if you were just being grateful for money.

I recommend starting with a smaller amount on your first cheque, and after you receive it, you can keep increasing the values of your subsequent cheques. The benefit of starting small is that when you do receive the money you asked for you will know that you made that happen, and this knowledge (or feedback) will demonstrate that gratitude works and that will make larger amounts believable for you.

Once you have filled in the details of the cheque, hold it in your hands and think about the specific thing you want the money for. Get a picture in your mind and visualise yourself actually using the money to get the very thing that you want, and put as much excitement and gratitude into it as you can.

Maybe you want the money for a website redesign, or to hire that marketing resource you know you need, or to buy a new computer, or put on that event you've been thinking about, or attend that training course you know will help you. Imagine yourself with the item, or at the event, or having completed the training, or welcoming your new hire on their first day. Feel as happy and grateful now as you will be when you actually receive it.

Once you've completed these steps, take your magic cheque with you today, or put it in a place where you will see it often. On at least two or more occasions during the day take the cheque in your hands, picture yourself using the money for what you want, and feel as grateful and excited as you can.

At the end of the day, either keep your cheque where you had it, or put it in another prominent place where you will see it daily. Any time you see the cheque, feel as though you've received the money, and be grateful. When you have received the money on your cheque, or if you receive the item you intended the money for, replace the cheque with a new amount and continue…

==============

PRINCIPLE FIVE: ALIGN YOUR FINANICAL DESTINY WITH YOUR VALUES

In the first exercise we did you defined your current hierarchy of personal values. Was there a financial value in there? If not then this will have an impact on your focus, thoughts, words and actions around money. So this needs to be addressed.

We are pulling together many of the principles previously mentioned to harness the universal laws here. Your value hierarchy is actively demonstrated in your life. How you prioritise and the things and situations you manifest tend to be directly related to your highest values. So if as a business owner you do not have financial success, mastery, security or independence as a high value, you are going to want to utilise the techniques here to bring this more into focus for you.

We will once again be utilising the work of Dr. Demartini by learning to use his values linking exercise, which provide a way to alter the order of your values, by raising one from a lower to a higher position, in a way that actually changes the physiology of the brain to ensure it embeds and sticks.

==============

Dr. Demartini has developed and utilised two very simple techniques to assist you via a combination of understanding the universal laws of gratitude and attraction and the physiology of the human brain.

Within your value hierarchy, if you want to raise any mention of finances – be that financial success, mastery, security or independence, you need to complete the following steps:

STEP ONE:

In a journal or in the space provided the exercise section, write **200** general benefits of building wealth and saving money, and how it serves you. Yes, you heard that right, two hundred benefits. With each benefit that you write down you are improving and enhancing the association in the brain between values and money, two hundred is chosen because once you get to this point you've become creative, you've explored all seven areas of your life and you will now start to see many more opportunities for this to manifest in your life. Don't allow yourself to become totally consumed by consumerism here. This isn't about just writing down all the things money allows you to buy – spending your money isn't what financial security or independence is about…. (NB this is not an easy task, it often takes days to get it done – just jot them down when they occur to you, but keep going until you get to 200…

STEP TWO:

Now it's time to get specific. In this list write 200 specific benefits of how building wealth will assist you in achieving your top three personal values.

Start by reminding yourself of your top three values (as distinguished in the first exercise)

Now link these. For example, if your top value is your children, then you need to think about how increasing your wealth will support the fulfilment of that value – i.e. education, health, home…

==============

Wow there's a lot of work there huh, but it is so worth it so please keep going! Even if you decide that business ownership is not for you, having a healthy relationship with money is a great by-product. Also, don't forget you can apply these principles to many other areas of life too. For example, if you want to put a higher priority on your health and fitness, you can use this exercise to bring fitness up in your hierarchy.

3. YOUR SELF-LIMITING BELIEFS

Self-limiting beliefs around your worth or deserving of success can block this 'I' Psychology quadrant as well. There are many self-limiting beliefs that we hold about ourselves. The same self-righteous/ self-wrongeous imbalance will be in place here.

Reading through the following examples, you'll now be able to tell that some of these are related to perspective, and using your Anchor knowledge you'll be able to understand why certain of these would be the thought process of certain anchors. You'll notice that others are a result of the imbalance and lack of fair exchange. There are even some more examples in there about finance...

- *I'm not somebody who follows through*
- *I'm good at starting projects but I can't finish them*
- *I'm not an expert*
- *Nobody cares what I have to say*
- *I'm not perfect. Why would anybody listen to/buy from/hire me?*
- *I didn't work hard enough on this*
- *I don't have time*
- *My family isn't entrepreneurial ("Smiths don't start businesses!")*
- *I'll sound stupid*
- *Somebody has thought of this before*
- *Other people can do it better than me*
- *Nobody is interested in my ideas*
- *My idea is weird. It's not the norm*
- *If I succeed, I won't be able to sustain it*
- *I don't have the skills*
- *Nobody would want what I have to offer*
- *I don't know enough*
- *The people who are successful in this are out of your league*
- *You're not going to be successful so there's no point in trying*
- *I'm too old/ young*
- *I owe it to others to always work for them*
- *I'm lazy*
- *I'm not original enough*
- *I'll look foolish*
- *I don't feel like I could give enough value*
- *I've tried it before and failed, so I'll fail if I try again, too*
- *I can't because I have kids*
- *I can't because I have fiscal responsibilities to my family*
- *I will always avoid pursuing goals that matter to me*
- *What is meant to be will happen*
- *I can't ask for anything, I'll be rejected*
- *I don't/wouldn't know where to start*
- *I don't have the willpower*
- *I'm not smart enough*
- *I don't have enough support*
- *I don't have the connections*
- *If I fail it will be disastrous, so I won't risk too much*
- *I can't because I don't have the experience*
- *I won't be able to have a personal life if I am the boss*
- *I'll seem too domineering and men won't want to go out with me*
- *My husband will resent my spending so much time away from home*
- *Someone else would do a better job than I would*

"Until we make the unconscious conscious it will run our lives and we call it fate"

— Carl Jung

So just to finish off this Quadrant, let's just make sure you're not leaving anything hiding in the background that could derail you. Let's do one last exercise just to exorcise the last of your self-limiting beliefs.

===============

EXERCISE – REVIEW AND RELEASE

One of the pitfalls of being such a therapeutically savvy culture is that we can often see where our problems come from, but then use that knowledge as an excuse to avoid moving forward in life; e.g. "I can't start a business, because I came last in the social enterprise competition at school when I was 14." While self-awareness is a vital facet of transformation, insight alone does not guarantee change. How many people do you know who appear to fully understand the nature of their problems, without seeming to be able to do anything to alter them? The essence of any true transformation lies in the letting go.

There is a time for everything, and not all of our challenges are meant to disappear just because we want them to or think that they should. Some problems must simply be lived with, and some simply lived through. Many, however, have outstayed their welcome and are long overdue for release. We continue to entertain them, however, because we've discovered that some of our troubles actually have their advantages. In spite of our protestations to the contrary, we perpetuate many of our dramas because we've found that they leverage sympathy, help us avoid taking responsibility for our lives, and give us viable reasons for avoiding risk in life without much chance of being challenged. In short, they become our comfort zone.

And so, we've grown attached to the very things we complain about the most. So attached, in fact, that we've even come to identify with them. We have been buried under the mountain of false beliefs, arduous expectations, and unresolved resentments that we've been carting around. Rather than see ourselves as innately capable, we have been frustrated by all sorts of burdensome attachments that have thwarted expression in our lives. In order to experience change therefore, we will need to release all that is keeping us out of balance in our lives, so that the possibility can begin to manifest itself fluidly and effortlessly in our lives.

We are standing at the crossroads, and we must make a choice. We can either hold on to the old ways, or we can jump off the cliff by letting go of that which is familiar. We are required to surrender those things within ourselves that do not serve us — not so that we can get something in return, but simply because it is the better choice for our growth in life.

Having the willingness to absolutely let go is the one crucial key to transforming our lives. Hence the stereotype of 'bottoming out' before one is willing to change, which implies that most of us are not willing to let go of our way of doing things until we've completely bankrupted ourselves.

Try asking yourself the following questions:

- Am I so stubborn that I must lose everything, and everybody who comes into my life, before I become willing to change?
- How willing am I to be inconvenienced? To be uncomfortable? To be wrong?
- How willing am I to surrender control? To follow directions? To take real risks where I might actually fail at something?

Wherever you've answered with a resounding negative, or even hesitated just the slightest bit, is probably the exact place that you will need to go in order to expand your opportunities for life.

When we talk about 'letting go' of our challenges, we are not talking about 'getting rid' of them. Trying to get rid of a problem is like the compulsive overeater who goes on a crash diet rather than deal with the underlying grief and fear that is driving the addiction. That approach, however, is us trying to deal with the problem at the level of symptom, rather than at the level of cause. Instead we must root out our false beliefs and the underlying fears that motivate our behaviours.

STEP ONE

At the top of a piece of paper, write on the left-hand-side, "I Release:" and, on the right-hand-side, "I Embrace."

Underneath the "I Release" heading, write down all those self-limiting beliefs that are standing between you and the possibility of being a business owner.

Some of these things you will feel completely ready to release today. Others, you will see as needing more work and exploration on your part as they perhaps feel more pervasive and deeply rooted.

STEP TWO

Now create a peaceful atmosphere appropriate to performing an emotional ritual. (Light a candle, burn incense, or put on background music that you love.) Take out the list of things you want to release. Now, on the right side of the paper, underneath the heading "I Embrace", write down what you would need to embrace to let each thing go. Write the 'counter-thoughts' opposite the things you want to release in order to bring yourself back into fair exchange, and release the block…

Example:

    I Release   I Embrace

(e.g., "I release procrastination and I embrace completing tasks promptly.").

Before moving into the next part of the ritual, take a photo or scan what you've written down so you don't lose the positive statements.

STEP THREE

Now, using a pair of scissors, cut the list across the page so that there is only one issue (with an "I Release" and an "I Embrace") on each piece of paper.

Bring your papers to a place where it is safe to burn them.

Speak each thing that you are letting go of and each thing that you are embracing out loud and then burn it

===============

"What has been full must empty; what has increased must decrease. This is the way of Heaven and Earth. To surrender is to display courage and wisdom." —Ralph Blum

Wow, this can be a very intense exercise. I actually do this each quarter, not just about work but about anything that I feel is outdone in my life, such as emotional connections or beliefs I've out-grown. I find it so freeing. In fact, my friend Sam and I tend to do it somewhere out in nature, with a nice bottle of wine and really put ourselves first and turn it into a ritual. It's great when we reflect on the changes that have occurred from quarter to quarter, it feels very transformational.

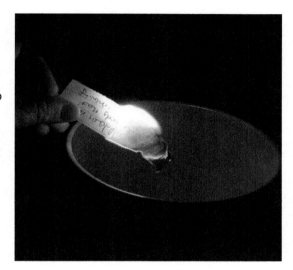

SUMMARY

Quadrant 1 done. This book is intrusive and intense as it's about getting real with yourself and getting under the skin of some aspects that may not be comfortable for you. This is all good as you need to be psychologically prepared and strong for what may come in the business journey you are about to embark on.

Having completed this book, you already have a whole host of insights into yourself that you may not have had before, that will stand you in a better stead moving forward. Understanding your values really helps you to be real about what you want in life and where your focus and energy goes. Your financial mindset is critical, especially as your business grows and you hire people – their livelihoods are then also dependent on your financial abilities. Lastly, carrying self-limiting beliefs is only going to make a hard journey harder, so releasing what doesn't serve you is a great way to lighten the load and enable you to live to your full potential.

Psychological strength is very important, as we will see as we move into our next quadrant, where we'll look at the Physical quadrant and the physiology of what it means to be a business owner.

 ## QUADRANT 2 – PHYSICAL/ 'IT'

In this section we are going to explore your physiology – your physical self and how this relates to your desire and preparedness to be a business owner.

In the Integral Theory diagram, I outlined three main areas we will cover:

4. **Stress**
5. **Resilience**
6. **Mind Body Connections**

1. STRESS

Starting a business is stressful. Do you really understand what that means and are you physically prepared for it?

To clarify this question, I first want to explain what stress is – the physiologically - in order to have you contextually understand why this needs to be considered and factored into your decision-making process.

Definitions are varied:

"Stress is the body's reaction to a change that requires a physical, mental or emotional adjustment or response." (WedMD)

"Stress is defined as an organism's total response to environmental demands or pressures." (Medical Dictionary)

"The reaction people have to an imbalance between the demands they perceive to be placed upon them and the resources they have to cope." (The Health and Safety Executive)

"Stress is a reaction people have when excessive pressure or demands are placed upon them, and arises when an individual believes they are unable to cope." (The Health and Safety Executive)

Regardless of the exact wording, we are essentially talking about something that is happening that is beyond our available resources. So great, now that we've got that…

The key thing to remember is that stress is not inherently bad. In fact, our ability to have a stress response is brilliant as it has meant humankind's survival.

Stress is primarily a physical response. When stressed, the body thinks it is under attack and switches to survival mode - releasing a complex mix of hormones and chemicals to prepare for what is necessary to survive. The modern challenge is that what our physiology perceives as stress is no longer the sabre-toothed tigers of our ancestors. It can now be the toxins in our air, the lack of nutrition in our food, the over-stimulation of social media or the stress of relationships. Our body doesn't differentiate. So before we take the proactive decision to embark on setting up a business (rated as the 15th most stressful thing you can ever do on the Rahe Holmes Stress Scale [11] – more on that later), it is worth really understanding what stress is, how you deal with it, and if /when is the time to take on more stress by choice.

To do this we're going to look at the following things related to stress:

1) Physiology of stress

2) Types of stress

3) Complete a stress test

SO LET'S LOOK AT THE PHYSIOLOGY:

The simplicity of the human body means that there are just three choices when it comes to reacting to stress – we know them as fight, flight or freeze.

	Fight:	Flight:	Freeze:
What we observe	Sometimes, when you feel threatened you can initiate the 'fight' stress response, which is aimed to ward off predators. So your heart races, your energy levels rise, you feel agitated and aggressive.	At other times when you feel threatened, you want to avoid the situation, removing yourself from the situation instead of tackling it. This is the 'flight' survival instinct. Recognisable also by heart racing as the blood pumps to enable you to run.	Or, like some people, your response to stress is that you 'freeze'. Be that at times when you want to do something that is scary for you (such as public speaking) or when confronted with something which shocks you which you don't like, such as seeing someone being attacked. It's a common response to extreme stress. To freeze you breathing shallows, your eyes dilate and your limbs become heavy.

Let's look at a couple of scenarios to demonstrate exactly what the body is doing and why it's a genius and elegant solution – or at least it used to be:

While out on the prairies, a caveman comes across a sabre-toothed tiger and in that split second the body has to assess the situation and decide which of the three reactions is most likely to save the caveman's life.

Can he fight and win? Can he freeze and hope to go unnoticed? Or, can he flee and get somewhere safe?

Let's say the decision is to fight, the body will then do what it needs to in order to optimise that situation. Blood will be diverted to muscles, shutting down unnecessary bodily functions such as digestion; while hormones, such as adrenaline and cortisol, flood the body, giving a rush of energy in preparation to fight. In short, the body gives all it has to ensure energy, muscle strength and stimulation are there to better the caveman's chances.

The pounding heart, fast breathing and boost of energy will be short lived but intense because, whichever way the fight goes, it won't last long.

Or let's say the decision is to freeze. Again, the body does what is needed to optimise that situation. This time a different combination of chemicals and hormones, acetylcholine and cortisol, are released, which means the energy gets 'locked' into the nervous system. This relaxes the lungs so the breathing becomes significantly more shallow. No breathing means there is no blood flowing to the limbs, which results in the limbs becoming heavy and lifeless. The body is aiming to have the tiger not sense the caveman and perhaps walk past him leaving him unharmed.

The last option is 'flight'. The same hormone and chemical mix as the 'fight' response occurs, but the body sends that energy to different places and shuts down different systems. We don't need to digest food whilst running, we don't need to procreate – but we do need energy and lots of if – so the endocrine system becomes catabolic, turning stored fat into energy to sustain the flight for as long as is needed, pushing energy into the limbs and heart to keep the legs moving and the heart rate high in order to run into the bushes or climb a tree to escape from the tiger's gaze or route.

These responses all seem logical and well founded. Let's now look at how this plays out in a modern situation. It's 8am on a Wednesday morning and you're stuck in traffic on your way to a 9am job interview. Which of those three reactions will best serve you in this stressful situation?? Errr……. Well none of them really! But those are the only choices your body has so it will pick one. To avoid that, you'll get agitated, frustrated and angry. Or you'll get deflated, apathetic and detached. Lastly, you may get creative, passionate and motivated. I'm sure you can relate these reactions to many situations you've found yourself in. The emotions and sensations in the body tell you which reaction is happening underneath the surface.

Not to say that these reactions don't have their place – they still help us survive dangerous situations, such as reacting swiftly to a person running in front of our car by slamming on the brakes. The challenge is when our body goes into a state of stress in inappropriate situations, like sitting in a car, stuck in traffic. When our physiology focuses on the reaction of stress chosen, it means all other functions are minimised. That can be a great hindrance in both our work and home lives.

If we are kept in a state of stress for long periods it is most definitely detrimental to our physical, emotional and mental health.

To understand why this is, we need to understand two of the physiological systems of the body - the endocrine system and the autonomic nervous system. Don't worry, I'm not going to get really technical here. It's actually really simple.

Autonomic Nervous System (ANS)	The Endocrine System
Responsible for the control of the bodily functions not consciously directed, such as breathing, the heartbeat, digestive processes, sexual arousal etc. It is controlled by the hypothalamus (a gland in the brain) and is broadly made up of two sub-systems – the sympathetic which controls the fight or flight response and the parasympathetic which controls the freeze response. The key difference is a response based on action/stimulation versus conservation/relaxation.	A collection of glands that produce the hormones that regulate metabolism, growth and development, reproduction, sleep, mood, among other things. The main function is to secrete hormones directly into the bloodstream. Hormones are chemical substances that affect the activity of another part of the body (target site). In essence, hormones serve as messengers, controlling and coordinating activities throughout the body. The key thing here is that there are two types of hormones – anabolic which repair, rebuild, and rejuvenate, and catabolic which breaks down to release energy for action.

I shall explain with the help of a diagram....

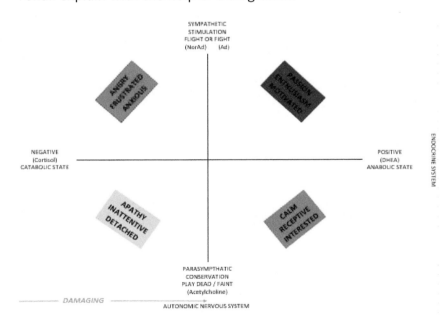

Y Axis - Autonomic Nervous System (ANS)

Sympathetic above the line, Parasympathetic below

X Axis - Endocrine System

Catabolic State to the left and Anabolic on the Right

I've put the chemicals on the diagram – you'll recognise most of them I'm sure, such as cortisol and adrenaline. Perhaps you won't be a familiar with acetylcholine and DHEA, but the key I want you to notice are the combinations. The way we know which combination we have is by the resulting emotions, which I've indicated in coloured boxes.

So if we have a fight or flight response from the sympathetic ANS combined with a catabolic endocrine response then we end up feeling angry, frustrated or anxious. If we have a freeze response from the parasympathetic ANS with anabolic endocrine reaction releasing DHEA then we feel content.

What this shows us is that the flight and fight response, when not appropriate to the situation we are in, can mean that we have a catabolic state (appropriate when you need to break down held energy sources to provide the necessary extra resources to fight/flight) creating damaging emotions on the surface and corresponding damaging internal effects.

While these stress reactions make perfect sense in many situations, in today's world this is less often the case. So let's now look at types of stress:

TYPES OF STRESS:

As stated earlier, the body doesn't differentiate when it comes to stress. If it thinks survival is at risk, then that's it, it calls it stress and responds accordingly. The entire system is designed to assess the world around us and judge it based on our intrinsic survival. That means the system is accumulative and this is where the juxtaposition of modern life and our basic physiology fall out.

We can classify stressors into four main categories, which are listed below along with some examples:

Physical	No exercise, too much exercise, bad food, excessive food, lack of sleep, exposure to toxins, exposure to chemicals, inflammation, illness, prescription drugs, illegal drugs, alcohol, caffeine, nicotine
Emotional	Jealousy, rage, anger, grief, fear, sadness, passion, lust, disappointment, which can be the result of relationship upset, family conflict, work issues, arguments
Mental	Depression, anxiety, worry, comparison with others, low self-esteem, self-confidence issues, over-thinking, catastrophizing
Spiritual	Lack of purpose, loss of life meaning, crisis of faith, disconnection, lack of compassion for others, lack of relationship with self

The lack of physiological differentiation between these types of stressors means that we can view them all as an inter-connecting series of buckets.

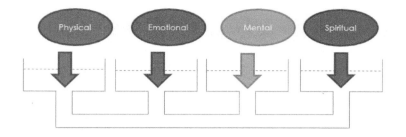

The body has a tolerance level, known as resilience, and it is when this level is breached by the accumulative level of all stressors that physiologically the decision over whether flight, fight or freeze is made. A great example of this is how you or I may react if we are approached on a dark street by a potential mugger versus how a professional boxer or marine may respond. They have a higher tolerance, as a result of their training and experience, for these situations so they may not trigger a stress reaction.

Advancements in our lifetime have meant that stressors are always present and affecting our physiology – be that man-made chemicals in the air, or in the soil affecting the nutrition levels of the food we eat, sleep deprivation due to noise or light pollution, electro-magnetic waves stimulating our brains differently, inflammation caused by different/unnatural forms of exercise, or inactivity thanks to the modern habits of the sofa-loving gaming generation. This is all before we even get into the other types of stressors that modern living has created in terms of confidence, self-esteem, comparisons, status, financial security, community, love and all matters of the heart.

It's also important to know that the body will assume that the situation triggering these responses is short-term – such as that scenario with the tiger – the caveman either survived and returned to what they were doing before, or they died. We've all seen examples of this on natural history programmes when, having fled from the lion, the gazelle escapes and immediately stops and starts feeding again as if nothing happened. We all feel like that from time to time – like when trying to explain a pain that's gone.

The challenge is that with the body constantly reviewing the entire environment for potential risks, along with all those constant stressors we talked about just now, we are essentially living in a state of chronic low-level stress, and in the process of our day-to-day lives we are using up most of the body's tolerance levels.

This is why we can find the smallest things stressful, because our tolerance level is already depleted. This accounts for the times when not being able to find your phone can sometimes feel like the end of the world, and at other times a lovely relief.

It also means that when we actually need the body to prepare us for a truly stressful situation, such as a bereavement, getting married, getting divorced, we can find the body lacking or under-resourced, which results in diseases or conditions like adrenal fatigue, burnout, ME, anxiety, being prone to panic attacks, depression, the list goes on and on… In fact, The Royal College of General Practitioners states that 80% of patients sitting in a doctor's surgery are there because of a stress-related illness. It's time to take this seriously.

In the context of what we're doing here – deciding if starting a business is right for you – having the awareness of what stress is and how it impacts us means you can be consciously aware of your stress levels before you choose to add more, and new, stressors into your life.

If you'd like to understand this a little more, then I highly recommend– Dr Bruce Lipton P.hD Check out a great video from him on the iaay website – via iaay/uk/resources.

I'm keen to ensure that you fully grasp this, so let's make this real...

STRESS TESTS:

There are many ways to assess your current stress levels. Lots of places offer free online stress tests that are quick and simple to complete and give you a high-level view of your current stress levels. These tests utilise various techniques to assess stress levels by measuring what we can consciously assess – our emotions.

These are my personal recommendations (go to the resources page for live links):

https://www.bemindfulonline.com/test-your-stress/ (This test will take 5-10min and has offers details about Mindfulness, as a way of lowering your stress levels.)

http://www.stress.org.uk/individual-stress-test/ (This test will take 5-10min to complete.)

There is one test that I want you to do today. This is based on the most extensive research and is called the Holmes and Rahe Stress Scale - also referred to as The Social Readjustment Rating Scale (SRRS). This research is based on thousands of studies on the accumulative impact of stress. As mentioned, the buckets all link up and the tolerance is what is key here. So Holmes and Rahe created a scale of the stressfulness of various situations and then by looking at how many of these you've experienced in a period of time you can see how full your combined bucket is.

Your ability to cope with the demands upon you is key to your experience of stress. For example, starting a business might be a wholly exciting experience if everything else in your life is stable and positive. But if you are setting up a business when you've just moved into a new house, or your partner is ill, or you're experiencing money problems, your buckets are fuller, and thus your tolerance level is lower and as such you may find it harder to cope with all the demands upon you.

This tool helps to measure the stress load we carry, and by knowing that we can then think about what we should do about it. So, let's find out your current score... (Please allow 10-20min for this exercise.)

EXERCISE – HOLMES AND RAHE STRESS SCALE

The exercise is available from the iaay website–you need to download the exercises: iaay.uk/resources

> Download Stress Scale Exercise

Okay, so now we know where we are starting from and if this is a consideration you need to be making in your decision about business ownership. Before we make that though, let's discuss possible ways of handling stress and, given what we have now know, what we can do to adjust our tolerance levels.

2. HANDLING STRESS & BUILDING RESILIENCE

WHAT IS RESILIENCE?

Different people have different abilities to manage stress, and individuals have different abilities to manage different stressful events. The key to understanding these differences is the concept of resilience.

Resilience is the ability to thrive under difficult circumstances. Resilient people can continue to act at their optimal capacity, even when circumstances seem to be against them. To be clear, resilience is not the same as coping; when we cope with difficulties we survive them, but sometimes at the cost of our own health and development. When we are resilient we find ways that allow us to continue to thrive and develop to our full potential.

Resilience relies on different skills and draws on various sources of help, including rational thinking skills, physical and mental health, and your relationships with those around you.

Being resilient does not mean that you don't experience difficulty or distress. Emotional pain and sadness are common to anyone who has suffered adversity or trauma in their lives. In fact, the road to resilience is likely to involve considerable emotional distress.

Resilience is not a trait that you either have or do not have. It involves behaviours, thoughts and actions that can be learned and developed in anyone.

HOW CAN I CHANGE OR ENHANCE MY LEVELS OF RESILIENCE?

There are five ingredients to resilience:

1. **Awareness** – noticing what is going on around you and inside your head;
2. **Thinking** – being able to interpret the events that are going on in a rational way;
3. **Positivity** – a positive view of yourself and confidence in your strengths and abilities;
4. **Help** – how we call upon others to help us meet the challenges that we face, because resilience is also about knowing when to ask for help; and
5. **Fitness** – our mental and physical ability to cope with the challenges without becoming ill.

1. Awareness

You can't change the fact that highly stressful events happen, but you can change how you interpret and respond to these events. The first thing to be aware of and accept is that things will never go 100% according to plan - change is a part of living. The second is that there will always be some things you cannot change, and accepting this helps you focus on what you can alter.

Psychologist Albert Ellis created a simple model for this, which he called A-B-C for Adversity – Beliefs – Consequences [12]. This model sets out a process:

Sometimes an emotion is so visceral that there is no time to go through this process rationally: you simply react immediately to the situation by running away, screaming, or similar. But your brain has almost certainly gone through the process subconsciously. The key is to practice tracking your reactions consciously as often as possible, so you can increase your awareness.

2. Improving Resilience Through Thinking

Having considered the elements of resilience, and the process of responding to situations, it may now be helpful to talk about what we can do to help develop resilience.

Here are a couple of useful techniques:

N.B. Any links shared below in the recommendations are also available on Exercise Download page at iaay.uk/resources

a) Gather More Information

You want to engage the rational part of your brain in your decision-making about a situation. One of the best ways to do so is to actively gather more information on which to base your decision. (Think back to Schroder's behavioural profile and the Information Search behaviour.)

Example:
Suppose that you see a snake by the side of the path. Your immediate reaction might be fear:

"A snake! It must be poisonous! I'd better run away!" [A-B-C]

But pause for a moment and gather more information. It might be dead. It might not be poisonous. It might be cold, and therefore only capable of moving very slowly. Oh hang on, is it a toy snake, so it isn't even real?

There are all kinds of reasons why you might not need to run away.

Your brain, based on your experience and your belief system, will present you with what it considers to be the most obvious explanation, based on its primal driver of survival.

But it may not be correct!

b) Alternative Scenarios

We're all prone to imagining the worst. It is also called *catastrophizing*, and it is completely natural. It's based on the brain's driver to survive; the same instincts that are creating the stress response are also working on a worst-case-scenario planning programme. This is clearly not ideal, but it is what it is. As we've established, in modern times, more often than not the worst-case scenario is not the one you need to be reacting to.

Examples:

Your boss asks to speak to you, and you immediately imagine that you're about to be fired. You get ready to defend your recent performance...

...but when you enter her office, it turns out that she wants you to know that she's pregnant and you're in line to take over her responsibilities while she's on maternity leave, with a consequent pay rise.

Your child's teacher asks for a quick word after school. You immediately assume that the child is in trouble ...

...but no, they just fell and cut a knee at lunchtime. No harm done, but the school has to let you know.

Recommendation:
There is a very easy way to deal with it, which involves generating alternative scenarios in your head:
1. Imagine the worst – let your imagination run riot. What could have gone wrong? What might have happened?
2. Now think about the best possible outcomes. How good could it get?
3. Finally, think about the most likely outcomes – probably somewhere between the two.

Now, make a plan for how you will respond...

3. Improved Resilience Through Positivity

a) Move toward your goals

Develop some realistic goals. Do something regularly — even if it seems like a small accomplishment — that enables you to move toward your goals. Instead of focusing on tasks that seem unachievable, ask yourself, "What's one thing I know I can accomplish today that helps me move in the direction I want to go?"

b) Look for opportunities for self-discovery

People often find that, as a result of their stressful situation, they learn something about themselves and that they have grown in some respect. Many people who have experienced failure, hardship or loss, have reported better relationships, greater sense of strength even while feeling vulnerable, increased sense of self-worth, a more developed spirituality and heightened appreciation for life. Think about the value-linking exercise you did in Quadrant 1.

c) Nurture a positive view of yourself

Developing confidence in your ability to solve problems and trusting your instincts will help to build resilience.

Recommendation: Complete these self-esteem/ self-confidence tests to see if perhaps you need to address this point as part of your resilience work. *(visit the resources page to access the live links)* https://www.mindtools.com/pages/article/newTCS_84.htm

d) Maintain a hopeful outlook

An optimistic outlook enables you to expect that good things will happen in your life. As Susan Jeffers says, "Feel the fear and do it anyway!" In fact, we will go a step further and invite you to not feel the fear at all. We want to get to the point where it's simply "So What, I'll Handle it". You have to focus on what you want, rather than worrying about what you fear.

Recommendation: Read Susan Jeffers' 'Feel The Fear And Do It Anyway'. There are some great exercises in there and it's a really fun read that can have life changing impacts.

e) Additional ways of strengthening resilience may be helpful

For example, some people write about their deepest thoughts and feelings relating to trauma or other stressful events in their life. They find the experience of expressing themselves, and getting the thoughts and feelings out of their head, to be catharatic. Meditation and spiritual practices help some people build connections to their calm inner resources and restore hope.

Recommendation: Here are two things I do to strengthen my resilience:
1. Good Times Jar.

Every time something awesome happens, I write it down on a piece of paper, fold it up and pop it in my good time jar. The things I write down vary, the main focus being that they made me feel good. It could be a great evening with friends, achieving something, finishing a challenging project, not reacting to something that used to trigger me, receiving an unexpected gift, - anything I am proud of. I also note down things I'm proud of in others. Then on NYE I open and read them all. It makes even the worst of years feel different – it's the little things that make you happy so find a way to remember them.

2. Stream of Consciousness Writing.

If I feel overwhelmed – by a situation, by an emotion, by a commitment I'm taking on - then I take some time to let my unconscious share where it is at. I love this as it's a non-judgemental flow, I don't think, I just open a word doc and let my fingers flow over the keyboard and see what comes out. It gives me a sense of relief, can help me problem-solve, helps me connect with why I feel troubled by the situation, and I often find it insightful as it is a good way to connect with one's intuition.

This is a great video to explain the process it's accessible via the resources page on iaay.uk/resources

---

You will become more aware of what is going on around you, and inside your head. These steps help you to apply rational thinking to the situation, climbing out of any thinking traps into which you have fallen, and understanding and rationalising your emotional response to a situation.

4. Improving Resilience Through Reaching Out

No man is an island, entire of itself.
Every man is a piece of the continent, a part of the main...
John Donne (English Poet)

There is no shame in asking for help. We all need help now and again, and many of us function much better when we are working with others. As we covered off in the early section of this book, as a business owner you are going to have to get used to asking for help.

A good part of resilience is knowing when and how to ask others for help. This doesn't always mean they have the answers, support can be as diverse as listening, brainstorming with or reviewing your plans for a second opinion, all the way through to distraction through shared passions or hobbies.

Accepting help and support from those who care about you, and will listen to you, strengthens resilience. Assisting others in their time of need can also benefit the helper too.

Recommendation:
Draw out a map of your support network. List everyone you think has what you feel you're lacking – knowledge, strength, experience, resilience, patience, time - whatever you feel the criteria are. It helps to feel you have options and to be able to see the flow, which may include where you think

---

5. Improving Fitness and Health

The final element of resilience is physical and mental health. As per the discussion we had about managing stress, your stress levels are impacted by your diet, amount of exercise and quality of sleep, which means they can also have an impact on your resiliency too.

a) Sleep quality

The importance of sleep should never be under-estimated – it is an incredibly essential time for the body – and in terms of regulating stress it is when the body goes fully into its sympathetic and anabolic mode – repairing, rebuilding and rejuvenating. The body will eliminate the toxins, inflammation and so on all of which is using up your stress tolerance load. So sleep is in many ways better for you than exercise. Very few of us get enough sleep, or enough quality sleep. It is worth educating yourself about the best sleep environment, understand how much you need and what times are best for you. There are even some sleep quizzes to help you assess if you're getting enough.

Links *(available on the resources page)*:
http://www.sleepcouncil.org.uk/how-much-sleep-do-we-need/
Do this sleep quiz: https://sleepcouncil.org.uk/thirty-day-plan/

"There is a founder myth that if you are starting a company you can't afford to get enough sleep,"
Huffington said. "But in reality three-quarters of startups fail, and perhaps if these founders were
getting the sleep they need they'd have a higher likelihood of succeeding."

- Ariana Huffington

b) Nutritional basics

The primary goal of eating – from a physiological point of view, i.e. for survival purposes – is for you to get nutrients into your body to enable growth, repair and energy production. In order for you to accomplish this goal, you must put food in your mouth and then be able to properly digest that food to break it down into the nutrients it contains, which can then be used as your body's innate wisdom sees fit.

We consume nutrients in all we eat - meat, fish, eggs, fruits, vegetables, grains and so forth – and your body digests and absorbs them and sends them to each cell where they are converted into ATP (the body's energy unit) via a series of complex chemical reactions. Every metabolic process in your body depends on energy, whether it is digesting food, thinking, making sperm cells, blinking, talking, beating your heart, breathing and so on. If nutrition is not optimal – meaning <u>what</u> you eat, <u>when</u>

you eat, <u>how</u> you eat – efficient energy production is virtually impossible, and for your body this is probably one of the most stressful situations it could imagine in terms of preparing for survival.

I am highlighting this as for many people eating is way down on their list of priorities. Due to hectic lifestyles, many of us don't focus on eating! This needs to change; if you want to improve resilience, decrease stress and move your life forward safely, then it is time to get informed and ensure you are eating well.

Did you know that digestion begins with your senses – thinking about food, seeing food, smelling food, hearing sounds when food is cooking, and touching food stimulates something called the cephalic response. The cephalic response switches digestion 'on', by which we mean flips the autonomic nervous system into sympathetic mode (digest and relax) so that everything needed for the proper digestion and absorption of nutrients is stimulated:
- Saliva secretion
- Stomach acid secretion
- Pancreatic enzyme secretion
- Gallbladder activity

The problem is that when your stress load is too high, and when you're rushing around, this response can't be properly switched on. In fact, the polar opposite side of your autonomic nervous system is switched on – the parasympathetic side - and as such the key processes above are not initiated.

How you eat determines how much energy exchange you derive from your food. If you rush around, put no time aside to eat, eat on the go, eat when over-stimulated etc - you are in parasympathetic mode and you are negatively impacting your digestive system's ability to process food and nutrients. This means you are impacting the means to overcome your stress load and repair, rebuild and rejuvenate your body.

I'm not about to turn this into a health and fitness book, so I'll stop this here, but what I will do is ask you to consider three things and provide you with some links to pick up this thread and continue on if you know this is an area you need to address. *(live links are available via the resources page)*

---

a) Mindful Eating. Dr. Albers defines Mindful Eating as "considering and balancing HOW you eat, and the WAY you eat, with WHAT you eat and WHEN you eat". It's about improving your *relationship* with food and eating.
   - http://eatingmindfully.com/learn/mindful-eating/

b) As food and water are literally the building blocks of what you see in the mirror, you literally *are what you eat*. That is however, insufficient, as you are also WHEN you eat and HOW you eat. Even more, you are also what THEY ATE! Quality of your food is paramount too! So it's time to get real about the quality of the raw ingredients you are putting in your body.
   - Think pesticides on your fruit and veg. If they are on this dirty list – go organic: https://www.ewg.org/foodnews/list.php#.Wb_qGMiGPIU
   - Think chemicals in your fish: http://www.foodmatters.com/article/the-most-toxic-fish-that-you-should-avoid or https://draxe.com/fish-you-should-never-eat/

- Think how the meat and poultry you eat have been raised and what nutrients they are really providing you, and be prepared to spend more and go organic so you are providing yourself with the best quality nutrients: http://www.natural-and-organic-choices.com/organic-meat.html

c) We are approximately 60-75% water, and every function of the body is monitored and pegged to the efficient flow of water. So water intake is of paramount importance. We all know that we die quicker from thirst than from hunger. So ensure you don't put your body into stress from dehydration.
   - An awesome book to read on this is Dr F Batmanghelidj's 'Your Body's Many Cries For Water'
   - No two people are the same, so to understand exactly how much water you personally require, read this: http://www.drozthegoodlife.com/healthy-lifestyle/body/a2283/how-much-water-should-i-drink/
   - Check the quality of your water – tap, bottled or filtered? http://www.naturalhydrationcouncil.org.uk/

3. MIND BODY CONNECTIONS

WHY DO I MENTION THIS?

Science is now telling us more consistently and robustly than ever before about the connection between our mind and body; and how we have the power to design and manifest our future.

We've already touched on this a little when we looked at stress systems in the body, I want to share a little more for the purpose of ensuring that if you do make the decision to start a business you do it in the most powerful way you can.

Let me explain.

Most of us will remember the physics we were taught at school – Newtonian Physics - and by and large we are all aware that over the past 100 years much of that has been disproven and now we understand that we live by Quantum Physics.

I'm not going to attempt to explain Quantum Physics here but I will highlight the key differences for you:

Aspect	Newtonian Physics	Quantum Physics
Who	Descartes and Newton	Einstein and Planck
Basis	Duality – Cause and effect	Non-Duality – Causing an effect
Connectedness	Mind or matter (discrete)	Mind and matter (interchangeable)
Controlling	External world controls internal world	Internal world controls external world
Energy	The force that moves things	$E = mc^2$, the fabric of all things
Our ability to influence	Pre-determined – actions don't matter	Nothing and everything is possible in the potential of the quantum field

Quantum Physics states that there is an infinite array of possibilities for each and every sub-atomic particle until focussed attention choses an option which then manifests. This is called 'collapse of the wave function'. Therefore, within the quantum field there exists a potential reality for any and every outcome. That's a complex concept to grasp but it's life changing if you can get your head around it.

WE ARE JUST ENERGY:

The physical body is nothing but an organised pattern of energy. We each broadcast a distinct energy pattern, or signature, which gives us our unique physical body and intellect. This is a representation of your state of mind, which fluctuates consciously and unconsciously on a moment-to-moment basis, based on your thoughts and feelings.

Quantum law states, "All potential exists simultaneously". Research completed by Glen Rein Ph.D at the Heart Math Institute in California [13] proves that we can manifest our intentions only when we have heightened positive emotions and clear objectives are in alignment. We now know the quantum field responds when wishes and aims are coherent (aligned) i.e. are broadcasting the same signal.

Thoughts – the language of the brain – are the electrical charge you send out into the field. Feelings – the language of the heart – are the magnetic charge you draw out of the field.

So it is only by changing the broadcast (thoughts and feelings) that we change the situation. If you don't change both - you will not get a new outcome.

What this tells us is:

> **"That when you hold clear, focused thoughts about your purpose, accompanied by enthused emotional engagement, you broadcast a strong electromagnetic signal that draws you towards a potential reality that matches what you want."**
> **Dr. Joe Dispenza**

THE KEY HERE:

You must focus on **what** you want not **how** you want it.

If you attempt to define the route to getting what you want by defining the 'how', you're trying to control from the external environment which means you've gone Newtonian – you're using cause and effect. Instead you want to leave the 'how' to the quantum field and cause an effect (i.e. a change and materialisation of one of the infinite possibilities). To do that, you need to surrender, trust and let go of 'how'.

Let's bring this to life with some examples shall we? As this can be hard to grasp, and it is easy to wonder where the what and the how meet.

➤ You're in debt, and want to be debt-free. So you need to hold a clear focussed thought of being debt-free – how it feels to not have the stress, to count the pennies, to have to say no to social invites. But you have to not define how you got debt-free. Instead, be open to all the many ways the universe can give you money – tax refunds, discounts, lottery, promotion etc. Be open to the route, but know the destination.

➤ You're single and want to be in a relationship So you need to hold a clear focussed thought of how you'll feel once you have a partner. The security you'd feel, the social activities you'd do together, the laughter, the joy. What you cannot do is transfix on a particular partner, or how or where you'll meet them – let the universe help bring someone to you that will ensure you feel that way every day.

I don't want to go too deep down this path, although I do feel it's a fascinating journey that I invite everyone to become aware of because it's our lives, our physics and so much has moved on from what we were taught at school. Two great places to start are:

> Recommendation *(links to these books are available on the resources page)*:
> Joe Dispenza, 'Breaking The Habit Of Being Yourself'
> Bruce Lipton, 'The Biology Of Belief'

It is useful to assess where we are today, and to gain feedback as we learn, which includes looking for feedback relating to where we are not yet getting the results we want, so we can address and realign to enhance the coherence and strengthen the signal.

PHYSICAL SYMPTOMS AS FEEDBACK

So, thoughts have energy and emotions have energy. We are all clear on that. They make you do and say things, and act in certain ways. They make you jump up and down or lie prone in bed. They determine what you eat and who you love.

The energy behind what you think and feel does not just disappear if it is held back or repressed. When you cannot, or do not, express what is happening on an emotional or psychological level, that feeling becomes embodied (you take it deeper within yourself) and it manifests though the physical body. Yes, this applies to trauma and tragedy but it also applies to us being less than 100% honest with ourselves; saying we want something, or we believe something and not feeling it, is incoherent, and thus the dichotomy will be embodied.

This makes sense when you think about the physiology we looked at earlier, about the autonomic nervous system (ANS) and endocrine system. There's more to add here, we know that the limbic system is the emotional centre of the brain. It includes the hypothalamus, which is the small gland that transforms emotions into physical responses, and it controls appetite, blood-sugar levels, body temperature, and the automatic functioning of the heart, lungs and digestive and circulatory system (as it's also part of the ANS). It's like a pharmacy, releasing the necessary chemistry to maintain a balanced system.

Within the limbic system also sits the amygdala and the pineal gland. The amygdala is a brain structure that is connected to fear and pleasure, while the pineal gland monitors the endocrine system and releases powerful hormones that act as painkillers and anti-depressants.

This indicates the intimate relationship between the mind, the endocrine system and the autonomic nervous system, demonstrating the connection between how you feel and how you behave; namely, between your emotions and your physical state.

Therefore, when we understand these connections it follows that your physical state can give you information to trace back to the originating thoughts and feelings. Often a physical symptom can give you a great understanding of the lack of coherence between the language of your brain and your heart and thus why things are not manifesting in your life in the way you would like.

There are two amazing researchers and authors in this regard, who I've used many times when I can't quite understand why things in my life are not moving as I want them to – I'll share two examples with you to demonstrate this:

a) I have had many different forms of Epstein-Barr virus over my life – be that glandular fever, ME, hashimotos thyroiditis, arthritis, chronic fatigue etc. – so I found it fascinating when I learnt that it represents 'pushing beyond one's limits. A fear of not being good enough and a draining of inner support'. That enabled me to assess what it was that was not coherent and address it such that I could move forward (with the added bonus of better health too). It was this that saw me leave the corporate world, having been honest about what it was I really wanted from life.

b) All my life I have had issues with my feet. They are the first place I get pain and I spent about a decade limping one way or another. Feet represent our understanding – of ourselves, of life, or others. Ask anyone who knows me and they'll tell you that I spend so much energy trying to ensure I understand them and am understood by them, I have always felt I'm not understood for some reason. I had to work hard to get to the bottom of what that meant in terms of incoherence but once I did, not only did things change in how I felt about myself, but also in how others reacted to me and how my business success improved - plus as an extra bonus, I can wear heels again!!

Before you embark on the stressful challenge of starting a business, you need to ensure you are coherent – so I would recommend you read one of the two following books to learn how your mind and body are connected:

Recommendations *(links to these books are available on the resources page)*:
Deb Shapiro, 'Your Body Speaks Your Mind'
Louise Hay, 'Heal Your Body'

GRATITUDE AS AN ENHANCING TECHNIQUE

Typically, we are grateful for what we **already** have – we rely on an external reality to make us feel differently internally (we go Newtonian once again). We must instead (to be quantum) give thanks for something that exists as a potential but has not yet happened. That moves you from cause and effect to causing an effect. When in a state of gratitude, we transmit a far stronger signal into the field that an event has already occurred.

Gratitude is more than an intellectual thought process. You need to feel as though what you want is in your reality at this very moment. Thus, your body (which only understands feelings) must be convinced that it has the emotional quotient of the future experience, happening to you now.

"Gratitude unlocks the fullness of life. It turns what we have into enough, and more. It turns denial into acceptance, chaos into order, confusion into clarity. It can turn a meal into a feast, a house into a home, a stranger into a friend."

- Melodie Beattie

Exercise: Daily Gratitude Journal
Every morning, before you get out of bed, write down 10 statements that start with;
"I am truly grateful for…."
And complete it with a current statement about your future intention.
i.e. I am truly grateful for the help my products provide to those that read them. I am truly grateful for how vital and well I feel every day. I am truly grateful for the unconditional love and support around me. I am truly grateful for the financial security my business provides for me and my family, enabling us to maintain the lifestyle we want.

SUMMARY:

I do understand that, upon first glance, this section may occur as a little odd to have within a book about business, so I'd like to remind you why I've included it.

Firstly, integral theory shows it is imperative to cover all four quadrants when considering how to positively increase the likelihood of a successful outcome.

Secondly, starting a business requires a lot of energy – both physical and emotional - so it's important to understand the physiology of that, and how you can best support yourself. I am a firm believer that knowledge is power and I assert that too few people understand the strength of connection between their mind and body – how stress is created, why it happens and how resilience is key to priming yourself for the stressors of everyday life, let along adding the stress of being a business owner on top of that. As discussed, starting a business is the 15th most stressful thing you can do in the world ever, and given what we saw about the low level chronic stress impacting our tolerance levels, that could mean starting a business pushes you over the edge – and we want this to be a positive life-affirming and enhancing experience.

So whilst this isn't about whether you should or shouldn't be a business owner – it's more about deciding when and getting yourself in the best shape to make the most of it.

QUADRANT 3 – ENVIRONMENT/ 'ITS'

In this section we are going to explore your environment – how the world around you impacts your desires and preparedness to be a business owner. In the integral theory diagram I outlined three main areas we will cover:

7. **Current work**
8. **Financial setup**
9. **Cultural expectations**

1. TO LEAVE OR NOT TO LEAVE

The big question for a lot of people that are considering starting a business is if and when to leave their current job…

From an environmental quadrant perspective, this offers several angles to explore because not everyone is in the same work situation. Some people will have a job, while others won't. Some people have the desire to set up a business but are restricted by debt, while others have more freedom financially…

Contrary to the stereotype of business owners being risk-takers who jump into the unknown to bravely start their business as soon as possible, and live off noodles whilst struggling, recent studies have suggested that business owners may be best served by easing into the process. The study, published in the Academy of Management Journal, tracked a nationally representative group of about 5,000 American business owners over 14 years. They found that those who kept their day job while starting a company were 33% less likely to fail than the ones who went all in at the start.

To highlight the link back to our practical work together, the researchers also conducted personality surveys, which found that those who did quit their day jobs sooner tended to be "risk takers with spades of confidence," whereas those who kept their day jobs "were far more risk averse and unsure of themselves." Or in our words, those with stronger entrepreneurial, service or challenge anchors tended to leap first whereas people with Security, General Manager and Lifestyle anchors tend to be more cautious.

What is really interesting is that this two-timing approach is actually representative of some of the finest people in business today; many of whom you will recognise, though often this aspect of their career is not highlighted as part of their business story:

 Phil Knight: For six years, Knight worked two jobs. By day he was a CPA for Price Waterhouse, and by night, hawking running shoes and building a company that would eventually become worth $25 billion – Nike.

Steve Wozniak: Even a year after inventing the Apple computer, he was still working at Hewlett-Packard.

 Sara Blakely: Sold fax machines door-to-door for seven years before making it with her footless pantyhose. Meanwhile, she was rejected by every company she took her idea to. Finally, her perseverance paid off, and that prototype – Spanx – made her the youngest self-made billionaire in America.

T.S. Eliot: The renowned author kept his London bank-clerk job years after publishing 'The Waste Land'. He subsequently found another day job at a publishing house to bring more stability into his life.

 John Legend: The platinum artist released his debut album in 2000, but continued to work as a management consultant until 2002.

Markus Persson: While working as a programmer, Persson built video games in his spare time. He released Minecraft in 2009, and kept his day job for an entire year before committing full-time. Minecraft would go on to become the most popular computer game of all time, and he would sell it to Microsoft in 2014 for $2.5 billion.

 Scott Adams: The renowned Dilbert cartoonist and author kept his job at Pacific Bell for seven years after his first comic strip was published in the newspapers.

Of course, the further along you are in the creation of your own business the more frustrating it can be to still devote 40 hours a week to a day job. But keep in mind that there are a number of benefits that having a day job will provide:

1) **TIME**
It gives you time; time to iterate, and time to approach your business thoughtfully. You won't feel the pressure to cut corners, and if you don't turn a positive cash flow immediately, you will still be able to remain afloat.

2) **RESOURCES**
Having a day job also gives you resources. This capital is particularly important if you are bootstrapping your business yourself.

3) **FLEXIBILITY**
Since you won't constantly be bombarded by the nagging idea that you gave up your job for this idea, and have already invested your resources on a particular iteration of the company, you will have more flexibility to consider your position and change direction if it serves you better

Having a day job affords you the opportunity to fail, as ironic as that may sound, and this sense of freedom offers a welcome space for creativity.

When it comes down to it, keeping your day job until you are cash flow positive is not only the safest, but arguably, the smartest decision you could make. You have the time and resources, not only to validate your business, but to turn it into a viable business with sustainable growth. You will have flexibility in your lifestyle. You will be able to pay both your personal and business expenses. Importantly, you will be able to take a more thoughtful, comprehensive approach to building a roadmap from where you are to where you want to be.

Don't forget that there are many types of jobs and ways to do this two-timing approach. Temping, part-time work, contracting, freelancing as well as the full-time employee all fall into this category

NOT GOT A JOB?

Now of course not everyone has an existing job – some may be wanting to start a business rather than returning to work after maternity or paternity leave, or because they've been made redundant. If that's you, then your environmental factors here are very different. So we need to consider the benefits of starting from scratch without the distraction of other priorities and a whopping 40-hour week dedicated to someone else's success. I'd like to flag that there are other options available, which are worth exploring.

Finding a non-engaging regular income to cover costs may be required, depending on your financial situation, (we'll come to that later) and your home life (next topic on the board).

Certainly this is what I did. I had vowed, when I left banking in 2012, that I'd never go back, but after I was left broke after a business venture went south I explored my options - by completing a benefits linking exercise I shared in Quadrant 1 - and decided that the path to my business vision could be kept on track with some contracting, which I could do in parallel to my own business. By linking the ways that the corporate assignment gave me the ability to help small business owners I was able to consider this as an option and make a conscious and empowered choice. I found it a liberating experience, especially as I was contracting rather than working there as a permanent employee. It enabled me to get out of the debts I was left in, and build a secure base from which I could develop *It's All About You* in a structured, interactive, creative way, without impacting my vision and creativity with day-to-day pressures.

Bearing in mind that my main career anchor is being of service, this linking exercise was key in enabling me to see how what I may initially have viewed as a sideways step was in fact just a short-cut. It would have been much harder to have gotten here had I been stubborn and insisted on doing this alone. The stress and pressures would have been increased and the timescale would have been delayed. Speed and stress were both factors that were more important to me than 'using' my corporate network to help me (we are not islands and asking for what we want doesn't always come in the way we want it, but open your eyes and the help is always there).

So that's one option, but let's also look at the scenario that assumes you have a home life that enables a direct shift, and sufficient money to cover you for 12 months – then what? 12 months of dedicated time, structured around a coherent and comprehensive plan that is balanced to ensure all quadrants are covered and you've taken into account your natural polarities, behaviours and anchors – wow a lot can be achieved in that time can't it?? That's a reasonable choice too, right? So what are the benefits of deciding the time is right and going for it?

BENEFITS:

- If you dislike your job, are not treated well or are expending more energy than you feel is worth it, then there is a psychological and maybe also a physiology benefit (reference our work on self-limiting beliefs, stress and energy levels due to mind-body connection) to starting your own business instead. That said, it is wise to not start a business as a reaction to a negative situation.
- Taking the leap will empower you to establish new limits in your mind. You will break the boundaries of your current comfort zone, re-defining what you think you deserve or are capable of accomplishing. If it's fear holding you back, when you take the leap you will eradicate that fearful thinking, establish new boundaries, improve your outlook on life and your ability to achieve on high levels.
- The pressure may cause you to become more creative. When you put yourself out on a limb, with a no-excuse approach, your natural problem-solving skills kick in and you're open to new ideas and are willing to try something new.

- Even if you're a safe and secure kind of person, not every life step can be carefully planned out. You'll never know if you can succeed unless you venture out into new territory. There is risk involved in doing anything new, but the reward is there too.
- Sometimes you have to trust your instincts. If your gut is leading you down an unknown path but inside you know that something big is on the other side, go for it! You'll never know what you can accomplish until you do something you've never done. Take the risk, you'll step into some of your biggest rewards.
- On a more practical level, you will gain total independence of your time and how you spend it. If creative freedom and a flexible schedule are things you enjoy, then you'll have a sense of personal satisfaction and the excitement of achievement.

These are a few of the benefits that come to mind, and of course depending on your personal psychology these may or may not appeal. The key here is that you are unique, so only you can decide what the right path for you is around this topic – but you need to respect yourself to consciously weigh up the situation, all the impacts and impacted parties (including yourself) before deciding what is most important to you.

2. FINANCIAL SETUP

In the 'I' quadrant, we looked at your financial beliefs and how these can impact on your business ownership journey. In this section we are going to look at some wider financial considerations that need to be incorporated into your decision-making process.

CURRENT FINANCIAL POSITION

You need to be realistic about where you really are financially, and what setting up a business takes. We've already looked at this from a time and energy perspective, the other resource that new businesses can consume, faster than you ever thought possible, is money.

It is estimated that a business that survives the first two years will go on to succeed, so it is wise to go in with your eyes open. Depending on the option you favour from the 'when to leave' section, I always recommend that you have available at least 12 months' worth of capital – be that your personal costs (rent/mortgage, living costs etc.) and your business costs (overheads, wages, marketing expenses etc.) available to you so you can manage the pressure without compromising your creativity and decision-making skills.

Later in the course we will do all the number crunching needed to ensure you are 100% clear on what those costs are, and look at the financial options, and ways to structure depending on your type of business (services versus products are very different) but for now, a quick financial setup review should suffice…

Download Financial Setup Worksheet

The excel template is available from the iaay website–you need to download the exercises: iaay.uk/resources

It is critical to closely and regularly review your personal expenditure. The uncertainty relating to income that can occur when you branch out on your own makes it very important to have a really good understanding of all the moving parts within your lifestyle expenditure – especially if that includes supporting a family or regulatory commitments like a mortgage. Staying on top of how your new business venture impacts your personal finances can help you remain realistic about what you can and cannot afford for both your personal and business needs and wants.

SETTING THE BASELINE

I would recommend that the output number you need is 9-12 times the total of the personal and business costs you clarified and calculated in your worksheet. Right now, that is more than likely a scary number and may seem a little too out of reach. You may feel tempted to consider trying to launch on a shoestring, either because you don't have enough capital yourself right now, or you don't want to give too big a share away to investors.

I would really warn against this, as cutting corners at the beginning will not be doing your idea and your passion any justice. As we explored in the early stages of this book, you are naturally gifted in some respects, and not in others. A consequence of cutting corners may be that you decide to do more yourself, which may involve you needing to go outside of your skillset. Which is not a bad idea per se – we all need to keep learning new skills – but realistically it will add time to the plan, and be of a lower quality. If that's okay, then great, but if you respect your idea, then do it right the first time. Cutting corners inevitably leads to a higher cost in the long-run.

On the topic of using investment to get started, remember that sometimes a smaller slice of a large pizza is worth more than 100% of a smaller one!

(We will come back this topic, in more detail, at a later point.)

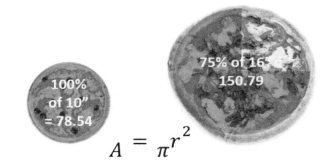

$$A = \pi r^2$$

100% of 10" = 78.54

75% of 16" 150.79

KEEP WORK AND PERSONAL EXPENSES SEPARATE

This might not seem that important, but it's one of the main issues that I see with new businesses, and it's a colossal pain-in-the-neck to sort it out later on. Do not mix business and pleasure; do not view your money as sitting in one shared pot. Make separate pots and manage them separately from the day one. Determine your company's expenditure and what's yours (as we've done in the financial setup worksheet). Getting these things locked down before you get going will save you a huge amount of time later on. And whilst we're on the subject of wallets, please please PLEASE keep, and record your receipts. Your accountant will love you for it.

POSITIVE OR NEGATIVE CASHFLOW

Another thing that's good to take into account at this stage is that different businesses are based on different cashflow business models; you need to be mindful of which model you are basing your business on:

Positive cashflow

A business model where customers pay for services up front, but where the costs for the delivery of that service are to be paid in the future. An example of this would be a cafe or restaurant, where you can gain credit from your food suppliers but get paid cash by your customers. Another example would be a consultancy or coaching-type service.

Negative cashflow

A business model where the cost of production is paid before the customers pay for services. Anything that requires the production of a physical product – clothes, shoes, candles, face scrubs, or an e-business where you need to write or record the 'products' before you sell them.

Ironically, the better a young business does in terms of sales, the bigger the hole it will be digging for itself if it has a negative cash flow business model.

I mention this as the differences will impact on the financial set-up that you need to consider in terms of what you need to have and when you need to have it by.

SUMMARY

This book is not about the financial side of business, so I've kept things short and simple for now. To summarise:

1) Get your current finances straight;
2) Be realistic about what you need;
3) Understand how the cashflow works in relation to upfront costs;
4) Keep your personal finances separate from your business finances.

By ticking off your list that you've got your financial setup sorted – not only will that demonstrate a maturity in your approach, but it will also provide you with a sense of stability which will positively impact both your psychology and physiology.

3. CULTURAL EXPECTATIONS

Whilst we all have our own personal views, we have to accept that they are at least in part formed or impacted by the cultural norms and expectations around us. Many of which are myths or exaggerated stereotypes. We've already discussed that each business will be unique, therefore everyone's experience of starting one will also be unique.

That said, it makes sense to be consciously aware of what the cultural norms, expectations, myths and views are, as you'll be opening yourself and those around you up to these pervading views, and will need to deal with the highs and lows of your business journey in the context of them. It is therefore best to be pre-warned; building your awareness and resilience around these, at the outset, will stand you in great stead.

So we're going to look at some of the biggest myths and expectations and get realistic about what it could mean for you. Whilst it is 100% certain you won't experience all of these, it's more than likely you'll experience some of them in some form. So taking a moment to give them some honest consideration now is eminently sensible. Pre-warned is pre-armed.

Myths or common expectations about starting a business:
1) It'll be easy – you'll be a millionaire in three months
2) It'll be hard – you'll likely fail - most businesses do
3) You need relevant experience to succeed
4) You'll need to work 24/7 and have no life
5) You need lots of money to start
6) You need to time it right
7) You need to be really tech-savvy these days to get customers – it's all about social media
8) You've got it have it all planned out before you start
9) Everyone else will have an opinion
10) Your situation has never happened before

1) IT'LL BE EASY – YOU'LL BE A MILLIONAIRE IN THREE MONTHS
Everywhere you look on the internet these days there are people telling you how they started a business and made a million in their first three months, *and they can show you how to do just that too!*

Well firstly, they are making their money off you so will say what is needed to get you to part with your cash. Secondly, they may well have found a niche that works for them in their market - with their unique set of values, passion, situation - but they will have generalised and made massive assumptions about who you are and your current situation if they claim they can replicate the same results for you by following their approach. If it were that easy everyone would do it – but the statistics don't back that up.

So yes, in some cases they will be speaking the entire truth – they will have done something that caught the attention of the market, and that's awesome – that's what we want but you cannot go in expecting that. It is neither realistic nor likely. It is always best to underestimate and be pleasantly surprised, than to overestimate and be devastated.

There is no such thing as 'overnight success'. No matter how you frame it, it takes years of hard work to become an 'overnight success'. Just because someone tells a story a particular way, or appears to have come from nowhere, this is never the truth and doesn't tell the whole story. The reality may be that they've been quietly toiling away for years – holding down two jobs, or this is their xth business because the rest failed – beneath the surface of the apparent overnight success, there's always a different story.

2) IT'LL BE HARD – YOU'LL LIKELY FAIL MOST BUSINESSES DO

Aha and the reverse – the stats say that over 50% of businesses fail in their first year, and that you need to be in business for five years before you can say you've succeeded.

People may well share things with you along these lines whenever you experience a dip in the road. Let's face it, there will be dips – success is not guaranteed, but neither is failure. The world of business is full of success stories, with people going from failure after apparent failure, until their dedication and hard work paid off and they achieved success.

You need to view the challenges as learning opportunities – don't get stuck into the black and white of business, of what you want success to look like or of your current view of what your idea has to be. You need to be willing to constantly review, revise and re-plan, and then get back to it.

3) YOU NEED RELEVANT EXPERIENCE TO SUCCEED

There are different perspectives to this, but by and large I would say that passion for what you're doing is far more useful than the experience of having already done it. Most elements of running a business can be mastered with common sense, can be learnt or delegated. Having passion, which will keep you focused and drive you forward, is something that can't be.

Going into a business you know nothing about means you can and will make some very dumb mistakes. You will soon discover however, that making mistakes has got nothing to do with experience; everyone – even the most established players - make plenty of dumb mistakes. They just make different kinds of mistakes. Perhaps mistakes born of arrogance rather than inexperience.

While it will never hurt to have some experience in any business you go into, for many businesses experience is not necessary, and you can usually pick up the experience you require along the way. Remember that you have already learnt so much via trial and error. You just break down the overall objectives and tasks into digestible pieces, and take each step at a time.

4) YOU'LL NEED TO WORK 24/7 AND HAVE NO LIFE

There's a very popular stereotype of the workaholic business owner, and yes, maintaining a balance in other areas of your life is probably going to be one of the challenges you'll face. There are times when you just about get the balance right, but whilst you continue to grow this rarely lasts very long before the next challenge disrupts things all over again.

The elusive work-life balance is out there, though many new business owners can't seem to find it. If you grind yourself into the dust day after day without relief, you're going to get sick and unhealthy, and that's going to affect your success. You don't have to work 24/7 to run a successful business. While you do need to work hard, and there will definitely be periods of serious intensity, you also need to balance that with self-care (good sleep, good food, plenty of movement), socialising and family time. These are very important elements in ensuring you maintain the physiology needed to be resilient to the challenges of life, let alone the added stressors you are choosing to add by starting a business.

If you're doing two jobs, then creating defined periods of time when you work on your business is key – but it can't be every night and all weekend. If you're not working, then you should make sure you set times for work and times for life and relaxation.

Being disciplined is key. We'll cover more of this in the 'Relationships with Others' section, as being considerate and available for family is important too.

5) YOU NEED LOTS OF MONEY TO START

We've already talked about this under the previous section, and as with the success dichotomy there are also polar opposites regarding the money you need to start a business. As previously described, a lot depends on the type of business: service or product; positive or negative cashflow model; if you have a job or not. There are so many variable factors, so don't listen to generalisation, do your work and find out what you need.

What is true, is that if you're not completely honest and realistic about your financial needs and capabilities, then it won't be easy. Every decision will be coloured by a financial lens. If you're always factoring in the financial component and feeling constrained, you may not make the best decisions. You may even come to resent your business if it impacts on your personal life in ways you were unprepared for, such as not being able to go to dinner with your friends, take holidays or go shopping in the way you used to.

This can be a great training ground though – to learn respect for money and to realise what is really important to you. Hopefully it will mean that when you do have money, you'll remember these tough times and be careful with your earnings.

6) YOU NEED TO TIME IT RIGHT

Here's another aspect where the advice is quite contradictory. There is as much advice saying timing is key as there is advice saying the only right time is 'now'. There is evidence for both, and you could argue it's a lot more to do with your readiness, in terms of resilience, realism and passion, as it is to do with the market and potential customers.

There are countless people who have started their businesses at the worst possible times in history, and the worst possible time in their personal lives. Entrepreneur and podcaster Pat Flynn started his first online business in parallel to receiving news that he was being laid off from his corporate gig and that his wife was pregnant with their first child. No one is likely to choose that high-anxiety period in their personal life to start a business, but life tends to take us where we need to go. And you could argue that the situation created the focus he needed to make it a success

Microsoft was founded in 1975, near the end of a recession, and later re-incorporated in 1981, just as the recession of the 1980s kicked off. These were two horrible times to start a business, but that hasn't stopped Microsoft's success.

On the counter side, Airbnb was told by countless investors it would never work and failed over and over again, before finally finding success during the recession as it captured people's desire and need for extra funds and was seen as an innovative way to enable people to still afford to go on holiday by renting out their house whilst they were away. It was only this combination of factors that enabled it to capture the market's imagination.

So the timing may never be right, therefore I would say that the most important factor – if you get to choose – is when you are ready!

7) YOU NEED TO BE TECH-SAVVY THESE DAYS TO GET CUSTOMERS – IT'S ALL ABOUT SOCIAL MEDIA

If you look on any social media platform or blogging site, you'll see lots of courses or tools to optimise their success, and yes there is certainly something about making the most of the platforms that have billions of potential customers on. But do I think it is an essential requirement? Well that totally depends.

It depends on the type of business you have; it depends on the business model you're working to; it depends on the vision for your business. If you are a sole-trader in a service industry that requires you to dedicate a large amount of time per client, then successful access to billions of clients would completely overwhelm your business, and time and resources may be put to better use by investing more in personal networking approaches, as referrals may be the best route for you.

If you're selling a product which you build yourself at home then, like the previous example, successful access to lots of clients could overwhelm your production. You may be better off with networking or physical store relationships. But if you have a drop-shipping affiliate business or direct sales then you can scale to your heart's content. If you're an e-business, then online ads and using all the latest gizmos and gadgets make perfect sense. It's about being relevant, realistic and purposeful with how and where you engage your audience.

This isn't a book about sales and marketing, but suffice to say the minimum you'd want now is the ability for any potential customer to be able to establish that you are a credible solution to their problem online, the rest is personal choice and marketing strategy.

8) YOU'VE GOT IT HAVE IT ALL PLANNED OUT BEFORE YOU START

This one might seem like an odd one to choose, given what this book is about, but I think it's a fair area to cover as you will encounter many different views on this topic. There are many variants of business planning, there are approaches that are very detailed, dry with a specific format, and there are other approaches that say you don't need a plan at all, asserting that you should just start doing it and figure it out as you go along. I'm a middle of the road gal on this one. I firmly believe you need to think through all aspects of what being a business owner means, I also think that if you over-plan, you may run the risk of restricting yourself.

It's a balance of preparedness and creativity. There is no one size fits all template that a business plan should follow, as every business is different. If you're self-funding then you don't need to create the same level of commercial model as if you're going to investors who will want to see things in certain formats, but it is wise to know the numbers. It's all about balance; you need to have planned out the basic framework and then you need to leave yourself space to evolve, to learn from mistakes and to see what opportunities come along.

That's for you to decide – it's your business. But you do need to have clarified for yourself what you want from your business, what you're willing to put in, and whether your idea can provide you with that. That's my minimum when it comes to planning, and luckily you'll have met two of those objectives upon completion of this book.

9) EVERYONE ELSE WILL HAVE AN OPINION

Your family and friends want the best for you, and for many the thought of starting a business is totally outside their comfort zone, which means they may question or doubt your ability to achieve it; for which you should read that they would question or doubt their own ability, and are projecting these worries on you. Others may be envious or jealous of your courage to do this, and may try to balance that in themselves by putting you down, or raising challenges for you to overcome. Again, this says a lot more about them, than it does about your abilities or likelihood of success. I'd be lying if I said I never got asked by friends if I was sure I was doing the right thing, if I was capable, if it wouldn't be better for me to stick to what I know I can do best, or to take the safe day job.

If you aren't strong enough to believe in yourself and your ideas when faced with constructive criticism, it may be time to consider your choices. When starting a business, you'll be underestimated by many, but this isn't necessarily a bad thing. I'd personally rather be doubted at the beginning and prove people wrong, than fall short of high expectations.

Conversely, I've also had friends who seem to think that I'm the bee's knees and want to big me up, exclaiming that every idea I have is just brilliant, putting me on a pedestal, from which all I can do is fall. While it may seem flattering, this response from friends and family adds unnecessary pressure too. Pressure to live up to their expectation of what I am going to achieve, what my success will look like and deliver for others. I find this far harder to balance in myself, but it is important that you set yourself goals that you believe are realistic, achievable and appropriate and live by those, not the false admiration of others.

This is your journey, and only your views are what really matters.

10)   YOUR SITUATION HAS NEVER HAPPENED BEFORE

It is amazing how good most people are at giving advice, and bad at taking it. It is very true that whenever you are in the midst of a situation if feels so all-consuming and personal that it feels like it couldn't possibly be like this for anyone else – even though when we hear others say this to us we shake our head at their naivety.

There will definitely be times in this journey that you will think you are the only person who has gone through this.

Let me be the first to shake my head, and assure you, many have gone before. Many have found themselves in the situation you will find yourself in; many will have felt as exasperated, frustrated, lonely, inspired, misunderstood, as you do. Many have struggled with the same decisions, challenges and opportunities. Many have followed a similar path (never exactly the same) and fallen, stopped or given up. Many will have found routes around and prospered.

That is the journey of being a business owner, and none of it matters if you have a passion for it, if you don't work hard for it, if you don't respect it. So, remember you're not alone, you're not treading an unknown path and there is always help to overcome whatever gets in your way – be that internal conflicts and indecision, or external challenges.

4. CONCLUSION

I hope that now we are three quadrants in, you are beginning to get the feel for integral theory and the value you can derive from looking at the decision to start a business from a really thought-through perspective.

Considering your environment and how that interacts with your psychology and physiology will stand you in great stead as a business owner – and set you apart from many others that have not taken the time to invest in themselves and their future business in this way.

Making a conscious choice about how to deal with your existing work, being aware and prepared from a financial perspective, knowing what may come at you from your environment, and really looking at it from your specific perspective, (rather than those of the general media, the public stereotypes or even your social and family networks) is critical to being able to stand firm and strong in your business journey.

We will now embark on the fourth quadrant; in which we will explore your relationship with others.

QUADRANT 4 – REALTIONSHIP WITH OTHERS/ 'WE'

In this section we are going to explore your relationships – your sense of connection with others – both in terms of the impact on them, and what you will need to assess as you pursue your desire and preparedness to be a business owner.

In the integral theory diagram I outlined three main areas we will cover:

10. Realism for family
11. Support network
12. Partnerships

1. REALISM FOR FAMILY

Yes, this is about you; yes, this is your business. That being said, if you are not single then your decisions have a direct impact on the lives of your partner and, if you have them, children - so it's sensible to consider how this decision impacts on them, and what you are asking them to sign up for, both in terms of the impact on them and what you need from them.

An interesting study, shared in the Journal of Business Venturing in 2016 [14], looked at three aspects of familial support at the start-up part of the business journey. They looked at three elements - social capital (in other words, emotional support), financial capital, and family cohesiveness - and the effects these elements each had on the success of the business venture.

I totally agree with their conclusions, which were that social capital is positively correlated with success, and strong levels of cohesiveness have an amplifying effect on that social capital, whilst financial capital is negatively associated with success. Let's explore this in more detail:

1) SOCIAL CAPITAL/ EMOTIONAL SUPPORT

Always remember that, just as you have your own unique combination of values, career anchors, behaviours, and passions, so does every member of your family. So you need to be able to explain what you want to do, and why, to them in terms that will resonate with them. This will enable them to understand why you want to pursue this course of action, and help them to see the benefit to them of it succeeding.

You also need to be upfront and honest about what you are planning to do, what it will take (in terms of effort, time and money), what you need from them in order to be supported, and what you promise to give them during that time to make it a fair exchange. For example, if you're asking your partner to do all the kid duties whilst you work two jobs for a year, you'll take every Sunday off as a family day, or if you're going to be using the garage as an office you promise to take your partner out every Saturday night. The balance needs to be specific to the values and passions of your partner and family to make them invest fully with their heart and mind.

There is likely to be less time available to the family, so you need to ensure you create opportunities for real quality time and you stick to it as rigidly as you stick to your business goals. The myth of needing to work 24/7, coupled with the physiological impacts of trying to do that, is something we've already discussed.

We've also discussed that starting a business is one of the most stressful things you can do, and that stress will impact on your family too. So ensuring they are aware, and prepared (i.e. resilient) for that stressful impact is also critical. Think about how you act when you are stressed; we tend to take our stressful emotional reactions out on those closest to us, even if they don't deserve it. Do you snap? Do you lock yourself away? Do you over-think and get anxious? What impact could this have on your family, and how are you going to avoid putting them in that position unfairly?

The main impact is often time, as time previously spent with family is now dedicated to getting the business off the ground. Sometimes as much as 75-80 hours a week is dedicated to the new business venture, which means a lot less of you to go around. You need to be considerate of their needs, while asking them to support you in yours.

2) FINANCIAL CAPITAL

Just like the adage we used in Quadrant 3 – keep business and pleasure separate. Clearly, if you are using your own funds to start the business you will need to have your partner really understand the budgeting process you've been through, and have confidence in your numbers and the ability to still meet the needs of the family.

The result is that often you are asking them to tighten their belts too. If you're going to be compromising for a period of time – such as cancelling memberships or holidays - they need to be on board with that. If it's going to appear to them like you're just spending money without anything coming back (negative cashflow model) then they need to understand that, so they don't panic unnecessarily and add pressure to you.

If you are going 'all in' on this business, then this is even more paramount, as if the business fails then what are the consequences? The family savings could be wiped out; you could default on the mortgage; it could impact on the future options for your children's education or your retirement plans. It is important for them to have an upfront understanding and explicit agreement regarding what extent the family assets will be put at risk for the sake of the business.

It can also become problematic if your family does not treat the business with the same seriousness as you do. If they see it more as a hobby or distraction, and nothing but a money drain, then they may employ a 'tit for tat' financial ploy. For example, when you buy equipment for the business, they feel they can spend an equivalent amount on something else, which places extra financial strain on everyone.

What I would highly recommend against, is adding to your start-up funds with money from wider family members, unless you do it 100% legitimately (which means full terms and contracts in return for equity or interest). The added subconscious pressure that having a debt to family, whilst asking for their support, is often enough to eat away all of your available stress tolerance. Then lo and behold, all your decisions are coloured by the financial lens, leaving little creativity or ease with how you make business decisions.

3) FAMILY COHESIVENESS

You will be surrounded by people of differing views regarding whether you should or shouldn't, whether you can or you can't. While you can easily dismiss the views of many around you, with family it is not so easy. The extra stress that can derive from a situation where your family members think the business is nothing but a pipe dream, or that you are better off putting your time and energy elsewhere, can make or break a successful business.

This lack of cohesion can create significant tensions, resulting in conflicts, resentment, and your feeling alone without support and encouragement from the people closest to you. From what we learnt in Quadrants one and two, that's psychologically and physiologically draining, stressful and damaging.

So it is advisable to spend the time upfront to really explain to your family what you want to do, and why it is important to you. Show them you are serious by sharing your plan and your intention with them. Make sure you do that in a way that they understand, which means speaking to them in their values. For example, if your partner has a high value on security and therefore may perceive what you're doing as risky you need to explain how doing this will make you more secure. If their value is around family time, then you need to address how supporting you to do this, will give them better quality time. This takes some thought, so plan it out, and be clear and specific about what you are asking of them, and what you're going to give them in return.

You know how some families make these wall art things that reflect their rules? Maybe you and family want to draw up a family contract to help you all invest in this process. You can detail specifically what you want from them, and what you will give them, you can articulate what is acceptable behaviour and what the consequences are for breaking the rules. If this is something that you think will help, then you can download a template I've used with clients here:

Click to Download Family Contract Template

The exercise is available from the iaay website—you need to download the exercises: iaay.uk/resources

4) IF YOU'RE SINGLE

Well if you're single, you could argue that a lot of the above doesn't apply to you. However, I would disagree. Whilst you may not have a partner or any dependents that require consideration and may add stress, doing this alone can be just as (if not more) stressful. I would still highly recommend doing the above with your family, (siblings and parents) as getting their buy-in to the process and the journey will create a stronger base; and let's be honest, if you fail and lose everything, it's probably them that will pick you up and get you back on your feet, so respect their love for you and engage them in this process.

2. SUPPORT NETWORK

We've touched on this already, so a short recap:

As a business owner you will need help and support. You are not an island, and you are not 100% capable of knowing and doing everything that is needed.

Support comes in many forms - intellectual, emotional, social. Listening, advice, distraction, mentoring, sleeves-up getting stuck in, or silent strength from a distance. All have their value and at some stage you will need all of them.

It is also fair to say that at some stage you will come across those in your life that:

- Think they know better
- Are envious or jealous
- Will doubt your abilities

It is imperative that you remember that this is a reflection of their internal beliefs and their views, often of themselves, that they are projecting onto you. Be prepared for negativity and for the pedestal, and remain grounded.

INNER CIRCLE

The best way to remain grounded, in my opinion, is to create an inner circle within your social network. Those you feel have the qualities to support you in the way you need, and the ability to understand what you're doing and why, so they can be sounding boards, without getting offended if you ignore their advice or take your stress out on them. That won't overwhelm you or leave you hanging when you need to vent or talk something through.

I have always found it best to have a range of people in this circle – perhaps someone you know who's also started a business, someone who shares your passion for the subject, someone who knows you inside out and how you think – never a partner though, as that can add unnecessary emotions into the mix.

For It's All About You, I had three amazing friends act as my sounding boards. Big shout out to Gregg, Sara and Brandon – you guys are my rocks! They are honest with me, they listen, then give constructive feedback, they build me up when I have doubts and bring me back to ground when I get carried away. They don't let me drift and they are as invested in seeing me succeed as I they were doing it themselves. Who's in your inner circle?

TESTING GROUND

The other way your support network can be useful to you in this journey, is those that you feel are representative of your ideal client. People who you would want to sell to. They can be great at letting you know if you are on the right track with branding, copy, imagery, ease of understanding etc. Every time I create a new webpage, or exercise, I always get a few people to test it for me and give me their honest feedback. Please consider if you have people in your circle like that – it's a great way for them to demonstrate their interest and support, and it's a free feedback mechanism for you.

THE SOCIAL SIDE OF LIFE

We've said in various sections that you cannot just lock yourself way and work all the hours to get this done, and it is the responsibility of your social network to ensure that you don't burn out or become a business bore.

You need to have balance in your life. So use your network to make sure you are still looking after yourself, still feeding your creative spirit, your physiological needs (exercise, laughter, food) and ensuring your inter-personal skills don't dry up. Be sure to make and keep your social commitments. Yes, money may become tighter, but a run or a walk in the park with a friend is free. Having mates over for a movie night, with a facemask or beer, is cheaper than a night out.

Whilst you're exploring opportunities for your business, and learning to say 'yes' to all opportunities that come your way, you need to remember to say 'yes' to the rest of life too.

FINDING LIKE-MINDED PEOPLE

It may be the case that you are not linked to other business owners or creatively-minded people in your social circle. That's okay – as we've seen time and time again, not everyone is.

It would definitely benefit you to have a specific social group that is like-minded though – to be able to reassure yourself that you're not going through it alone, that what you're experiencing is normal and there are ways through it. A problem shared is a problem halved and all that.

There are lots of ways to do this. There are many meetups and groups for business owners – start by checking out these sites *(live links are available on the resources page)*:

UK	US/ rest of world
https://www.meetup.com/find/career-business/	https://www.eonetwork.org/
http://www.wibn.co.uk/	https://founderscard.com/#events
http://www.fsb.org.uk/	https://www.startupgrind.com/events/
http://www.britishchambers.org.uk/business/events/	

Find somewhere you live, by simply googling = business start-up groups, or check facebook.

I was part of a business mastermind type group – which was my strength, especially during tough times of the business journey. We met once a month to talk about our experiences, and our group leader brought in speakers and led us in helpful exercises. We found, as the months passed, that any challenge one of us was facing, another of us had been there, and we were able to provide both emotional and tangible support to help overcome that challenge. Like being on an assault course and needing help over the climbing wall, some above pulling you up, others beneath pushing you up, that's support the nature of support (and the mud, and the dizzying drop down on the other side - that captures what being a business owner feels like sometimes).

3. PARTNERSHIPS

In the first part of this book, we talked about understanding what you bring to the business in terms of your natural and learnt strengths, and how this prepares you for being a business owner. Within that it was clear that there are areas that aren't your strength, and things that you won't enjoy or be good at within the business. We can now explore what that means in terms of relationships with others, not from a support perspective, but from a partnership or working with perspective.

Having been a business owner on my own, as well as having worked in different types of partnership, I can quite honestly say there are pros and cons to all options. This isn't about guiding you to make a specific decision, it's about ensuring that you are aware of the options and can factor all the possibilities into the decision-making process you're going through, based on consciously thought-through opinions.

TYPES OF PARTNERSHIPS

Given where you are in the journey, I wanted to raise four types of partnerships that may be relevant to you as you progress. Again we're only looking very high-level here to whet your appetite and inform your thinking.

The four types of partnership are:

Business Partners

Joint Venture Partners

Affiliate Partners

MLM/ Network Partners

1) BUSINESS PARTNERS

For many, the thought of starting a business solo seems scary, but having a partner makes it seem possible, even exciting. The thought of sharing the workload, the responsibility, the decisions, the stress. The ability to have two minds to think things through, to bounce ideas off, two sets of skills to cover the workload, two networks to help get things going, there are many, many good reasons why a partnership can be beneficial.

There are many successful business partnerships that have stood the test of time, be that a year or a decade. A few well known example are: Google, with Larry Page and Sergey Brin, who have been together since 1998; Ben Cohen and Jerry Greenfield, otherwise known as Ben & Jerry's Ice cream, who have been going strong since 1978. [15]

Then there are those that, much like a marriage, begin with enthusiasm and high expectations, only to end in acrimony and legal proceedings. Eduardo Saverin and Mark Zuckerberg's fall-out over Facebook is a great example. Another example would be Rupert Murdoch and Richard Li's attempt to extend News Corporation to Asia.

It's therefore important to objectively consider the pros and cons, and to think about what the partnership is for, and what it brings you/ them/ the business

PROS AND CONS

Sole Proprietor [16]		Business Partner	
Pro	**Con**	**Pro**	**Con**
➤ Minimal legal costs to set up	➤ Held personally liable for the debts and obligations of the business	➤ Easy to establish and start-up costs are low	➤ Partners are 'jointly and severally' liable for debts
➤ Few formal business requirements	➤ Risk extends to any liabilities incurred as a result of acts committed by employees of the company	➤ Potentially more capital is available for the business if partners equally invest	➤ Partners are agents and are liable for actions by the others
➤ Sale or transfer can take place at your sole discretion		➤ Greater borrowing capacity for start-up investment	➤ Every decision needs to be made jointly, or delegation needs to be agreed in advance
➤ Complete control and decision-making power over the business.	➤ All responsibilities and business decisions fall on shoulders	➤ Limited external regulation	
➤ Complete control over the strategy and direction for the business	➤ More challenging to get external Investors	➤ Easy to change legal structure if circumstances change	➤ The direction, purpose and strategy needs to be agreed
		➤ Two heads (or more) are better than one	➤ Compromises may be uncomfortable
		➤ Double the intelligence, skills and network capacity	

If the business partner list of pros suggest that route may be preferable, or perhaps you've already started this journey with a partner in mind or on board, then you need to take the emotion out of the situation, and get real.

This is business and, as I've said several times, business and personal matters need to be kept separate. With a purely business head on, it's important to know as much as possible about a potential partner - including how his or her finances and family life may affect the business, just as how yours will affect them - before signing on the dotted line.

Here are some questions [17] to ask before deciding if partnering in business is a good idea:

1. What do I need from a business partner?
You should look for a business partner who brings something different to the table than you do. If you're creative, maybe you need a more detail-oriented partner. If you have money to invest in the business, you may want to look for a partner with access to a market, or with great connections. Or if you're shy, you might need a good 'people person' to balance the equation. Sure, if someone is quite similar to you it may be more comfortable, but it may not be what you need. They also need to want the same things as you do – be that to build and sell, or focus on service or profit.

2. What is your potential partner's financial situation?
It is important to have an understanding of someone's financial status and commitments before getting into a venture together. This isn't necessarily an easy conversation, but in the same way that you need to be thorough in understanding your needs and agreeing that with your family, you need to that with a potential business partner.

3. What are the potential partner's expectations on the time involved?
Partners don't have to dedicate the same amount of time to the business, but it is important that they are on the same page regarding each other's expected time commitments. How many hours a day does your partner expect to put into the venture, and do their expectations meet yours? Depending on what you're each bringing, and what you agree upon, (maybe you're leaving your job and they are keeping theirs) the age old adage that it's better to under-promise and over-deliver, applies here.

4. Is your potential partner's commitment to the business as strong as yours?
A partnership can start off with fun and excitement, but within a short time the slog of every day can catch up with each of you. If you are not both equally committed to the business, and don't see the same future, then when the honeymoon wears off the extra stress will kick in, and such a change can be damaging. You also need to be clear that you both want the same things for and from your business. A shared vision is essential, and without it conflict will incur before too long.

5. How would they handle stress?
It's important to know what your potential business partner will do if their back is up against the wall - and rest assured it will happen. In the same way that you've had an honest look at yourself, you also need to know that you can handle how they react, and that they can handle you. If they've been in business before, then learning about how they dealt with

those previous situations is a good way to gain valuable insight. Did they bend the rules, put their staff or themselves first? Did they always honour their word whatever it took – and how does their approach match yours?

6. Do you trust them?

If you've known this person a long time, worked with them for example, you will know how they operate and have personal first-hand experience of whether their words match their actions. But if not, then you need to ensure that you have evidence that their word is what actually manifests. You are creating something that is a representation and reflection of you, so you need to know who you are bringing something into the world with. You need to be able to trust them with this like you'd trust them with your children.

7. Are they willing to put everything in writing?

Many partnerships between 'good and honourable people' are cemented with a handshake, but this is 100% a recipe for disaster. It's crucial to put it on paper - not only what is expected of each partner, but the consequences if expectations are not met. It is sensible to take the emotion out of it and agree with total clarity the boundaries and ways of working up front.

MY PERSONAL VIEW

I find this a challenging dilemma; I find the two sides to be very evenly balanced. I really like the idea of having a partner – of bringing something to life together – I know my strengths and weaknesses, and I feel I work best when someone is pushing me to be the best version of myself. That has been my experience. Yet my experience also showed the devastating effects when the partners' visions and interests diverge on the journey – and that was more challenging than anything I could possibly have imagined (despite having gone in with our eyes wide open, ensuring all the legal aspects had been covered). Our saving grace was that we were not equal partners (which means in deadlock, or when the compromises no longer work, the higher equity partner wins) and that simplicity was key to a fair and friendly ending of the partnership.

2) JOINT VENTURE PARTNERS

A joint venture is when two or more businesses pool their resources and expertise to achieve a particular goal. They also share the risks and rewards of the enterprise.

Businesses may form a joint venture for many reasons, including business expansion, new product development or moving into new markets, particularly overseas.

Forming a joint venture can offer unique benefits for some businesses. A joint venture could give you:

- more resources
- greater capacity
- increased technical expertise
- access to established markets and distribution channels

Entering into a joint venture is a major decision. There are varying types, along with the corresponding benefits and risks of such partnerships.

TYPES OF JOINT VENTURE [18]:

1. Limited co-operation
This is when you agree to co-operate with another business in a limited and specific way. For example, a small business with an exciting new product might want to sell it through a larger company's distribution network. The two partners could agree a contract setting out the terms and conditions of how this would work.

2. Separate joint venture business
This is when you set up a separate joint venture business, possibly a new company, to handle a particular contract. A joint venture company like this can be a very flexible option. The partners each own shares in the company and agree how they should manage it.

JOINT VENTURE - BENEFITS AND RISKS

This type of partnership usually offers great advantages, but it can also present certain risks, since arrangements of this sort are generally highly complex.

The benefits of joint ventures
A joint venture can help your business grow faster, increase productivity and generate greater profits. A successful joint venture can offer:
- access to new markets and distribution networks
- increased capacity
- sharing of risks and costs with a partner
- access to greater resources, including specialised staff, technology and finance

Joint ventures often enable growth without having to borrow funds or look for outside investors. You may be able to:
- use your joint venture partner's customer database to market your product
- offer your partner's services and products to your existing customers
- join forces in purchasing, research and development

A joint venture can also be very flexible. For example, a joint venture can have a limited life span and only cover part of what you do, thus limiting the commitment for both parties and the business' exposure.

The risks of joint ventures
Partnering with another business can be complex. It takes time and effort to build the right business relationship.

Problems are likely to arise if:
- the objectives of the venture are not clearly communicated to everyone involved
- the partners have different objectives for the joint venture
- the partners bring in different levels of expertise, investment or assets into the venture

- different cultures and management styles result in poor integration and co-operation
- the partners don't provide sufficient leadership and support in the early stages

Success in a joint venture depends on thorough research and analysis of aims and objectives. For the venture to work, you should effectively communicate the business plan to everyone involved.

CHOOSING THE RIGHT TYPE OF JOINT VENTURE

To help you decide what form of joint venture is best for you, you should consider if you want to be involved in managing it. Consider what might happen if the venture goes wrong and how much risk you want to accept. You should carry out the appropriate due diligence when choosing the right joint venture partner. You want someone who shares at least some of your values, and potentially has a complimentary anchor or set of skills, this means you assist rather than clash with each other, and are aiming for the same place and communicating in a shared understanding and language.

You will need a clear legal agreement setting out how the joint venture will work and how you will share any income.

PROTECTING YOUR BUSINESS IN A JOINT VENTURE

For some, particularly if they have an innovative new product to distribute, this option can be a good way to speed up the process and gain quick entry to markets. If this is an option you'd consider, taking appropriate legal advice to help really understand if this is your best option is essential. The way you set up your joint venture affects how you run it and how any profits are shared and taxed. It also affects your liability if the venture goes wrong.

Normally, each party will have to sign a confidentiality or a non-disclosure agreement. You may also want to consider signing a memorandum of understanding early on in the negotiations. This represents a commitment to the deal and agreement in principle on the main points.

MY PERSONAL VIEW

I am a great fan of joint ventures; I feel that if the two sides are clear on what they want and how it benefits both, and it is all done above board, then they can be very successful. At a start-up level it can be hard to find a partner who will see you as credible, so it may not be a strategy you can deploy in year one, but if you take the long-game approach and agree that you can prove your product or service, then it's imminently possible.

3) AFFILIATE PARTNERS [19]

Essentially, affiliate partners have a marketing/sales relationship whereby a business pays a commission to another business, known as affiliates, for referring new business to them. It's a marketing strategy that is performance-based, which means affiliates only get paid when their promotional efforts result in a transaction.

WHO ARE AFFILIATES?

Affiliates can be any manner of business, but generally they tend to be online in nature, such as bloggers or other content sites related to the industry, or sharing the same profile of client (direct affiliates or complementary affiliates).

The affiliate works to introduce their network (clients, potential clients, email list, facebook followers, twitter followers) to the merchant's brand. They might write a post about a new product or promotion on the merchant's site, feature banner ads on their site that drive people to the merchant's site, or offer visitors a special coupon code. If people come from that affiliate's site and make a purchase, that affiliate gets paid a fee.

Traditionally, many affiliate programmes were comprised of coupon and loyalty sites. As the industry matured, content bloggers came to take a more prominent place in many programmes. Innovative programmes are stretching the definition of an affiliate even more, partnering with schools, non-profits, and individual professionals.

AFFILIATE PAYMENTS

One of the reasons affiliate marketing can provide a higher ROI (return on investment) than other channels is because it's performance-based. Businesses only pay for actual customers, not just clicks or visits. This gives affiliates a big advantage over other channels from a pure marketing perspective, where it's easy to spend a ton of money on clicks without producing any actual conversions.

NETWORKS AND MANAGEMENT

Most businesses, if they have an affiliate programme set up, are well organised and administered as it can be a very cost effective way to expand the business with limited marketing spend. Although it is necessary to have the means to track and pay the commissions efficiently

As this is more often than not done online, they can make sure of technical features on e-commerce sites and use cookies to track a customer's progress from the affiliate's website through to the merchant's shopping cart. This enables automatic payment of commissions to affiliates based on the rules set by the merchant.

If managing this sounds like hard work, you can even delegate this aspect as the industry is now so well advanced that there are external agencies that can run it for you. Whichever way you do it, the key is to recruit quality affiliates, ensure they are engaged, find ways for them to promote you, and value the ones that bring in incremental revenue.

BEING AN AFFILIATE

Then there's the choice to be an affiliate and to derive some extra income that way. Think along the lines of Amazon Associates, you get paid not only on the product you link to on your site, but anything else in their basket when they purchase it.

As you work through your business plan, it is worth considering which resources would aid your clients that you could make it easy for them to purchase through you, and get an affiliate kickback. Likewise, think of areas of complimentary alignment that you could affiliate partner with to better serve your clients. For example, I've shared some personality tests with you in this book, I could share more in-depth ones with you if I were to set up an affiliate relationship with an online training company.

IT'S YOUR REPUTATION

The key things to remember here are that if you are promoting a product or service to your client, you are essentially endorsing it, so you need to be comfortable with the quality of the product and the associated company. If your clients use it, it is on your recommendation, so you may need to be prepared for them to come back to you with any issues. So do your due diligence on the company and ensure you'd buy it, and have fully tested it, before you recommend it to anyone else.

4) MLM/ NETWORK PARTNERS [20]

We all know examples of network marketing – Avon, Ann Summers, Herbalife, Utility Warehouse. In fact, globally there are more than 100 million people involved in a network marketing scheme, and the industry generates over £150 billion in total worldwide sales. In the UK alone, there are more than 400,000 people running businesses from home, normally on a part-time basis. So it's definitely an option if you want to 'be your own boss' but you're not the creative type and so don't have a real idea yourself and you'd like someone else to do the product development and marketing, leaving you to be creative with how you do the selling.

Not only are 'home businesses' or 'MLM's' very interesting, they are successful. Many long standing organisations have this business model, despite the constant supposition in the media that they are pyramid schemes.

WHAT IS MLM?

MLM (Multilevel marketing) companies employ a network of independent salespeople who sell products directly to people in their community. These salespeople earn income based on their personal sales, as well as the sales of people they recruit to work for the company.

So it is basically their marketing strategy – but it does mean you have autonomy and are self-employed. It also enables you to create recurring revenue from your downline, which can increase your income above your personal efforts.

Most commonly, the salespeople are expected to sell products directly to consumers by means of relationship referrals and word-of-mouth marketing, but this is changing with people creating online sites and e-commerce stores to assist them and take advantage of the technology explosion and online social media markets.

WHAT SORTS OF THINGS ARE SOLD VIA MLM?

Pretty much everything. Many of the household names in the multilevel marketing industry, like Avon or Nu Skin sell cosmetics and skincare products. Then there are homewares, such as candles, tupperware and cookware. Insurance and utilities are now a big one in the UK. In fact, you name it and there will be an MLM that sells it. Food, vitamins, wellness products, energy drinks, weight loss bars and shakes are sold by Herbalife. Even exercise is now available via MLM; take Beachbody, the company behind Tony Horton's fitness craze P90x.

In the two years after Beachbody created a multilevel marketing division using 'Team Beachbody coaches', its sales spiked more than 60%. So if you have a passion you can probably find an existing company that is related and set up a business with less hassle!

SO IS IT WORTH IT?

Critics warn that the model is unsustainable. If you recruit all of your friends and network to sell the same product, won't you eventually run out of customers? Which accounts for why people are getting creative with their sales approaches.

Industry supporters say that MLM presents a viable full-time business opportunity for those who put in full-time hours and effort. but most salespeople only work part-time to make extra cash, or to get a discount on their favourite product.

Whilst it has a lower start-up cost compared to a traditional business, it certainly isn't free or stress-free. There are a lot of out-of-pocket expenses, and if you're not careful they can quickly add up.

There tend to be registration fees, you need to purchase inventory upfront (often at very discounted rates but that's still a negative cashflow model), welcome kits, pay for and attend training seminars, marketing materials and product parties for example. Most companies have a laundry list of requirements, including sales quotas, that must be met to stay 'active' and if you don't sell them you often buy them to keep yourself eligible for the coveted commission kickers.

MY PERSONAL VIEW

I include details of this option as I've worked with clients on some very interesting and creative ways to really work the model using modern technology and sales approaches. So it's certainly an option for those who have a great loathing for all things administration and want to be able to really focus on the sales side of business. Or it's at least worth a consideration at this stage in the process, especially for people that have an existing network that they can utilise for sales opportunities.

SUMMARY

Your business is more than you. You need to be prepared for the impact on your nearest and dearest, and it is wise to get really honest with them about what you're doing, why and what you need from them.

It is also important to make sure you are a little selfish in thinking about what you need to support yourself. Does your social network provide you with like-minded people? Do you have a strong inner circle?

Be sure to take the opportunity to think about if you want to do this alone, or not, if you think that finding a partner in some way – all in, marketing at your lead or theirs, or a MLM approach (I call this semi-business ownership) – will be beneficial.

And that completes the fourth quadrant. Wow you've done so well – it's really special to dig this deep and very uncommon to be so thorough, but with this kind of decision, it is so important to do.

RECAP ON INTEGRAL THEORY

At the start of this book, I outlined integral theory and why we were using it to assist us in the answering of the question: 'What is needed to make the decision to be a business owner?'

We've now been through each of the four quadrants to explore some key aspects within each, and to challenge your thinking or expand your awareness so that you make this decision with a conscious, objective and rational mind.

Value Hierarchy Limiting Beliefs Financial Beliefs			Resilience	Impacts of Stress Mind Body Relationship
Psychology	**I**	**It**		**Physical**
Relationship With Others	**We**	**Its**		**Environment**
Family Support Network Partnerships			Financial Setup	Current work Cultural Expectations

So now it's time…

If you recall the basic tenants of integral theory, you'll recall that all four quadrants interlink and impact on each other.

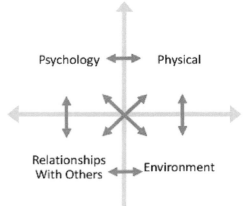

You want to make sure that you have considered the contents of each quadrant, and only if you are able to positively affirm that you are aware of and have a rational plan for challenges in each quadrant, should you now take the time to consider the question and answer it for yourself.

"Am I ready and able to be a successful business owner?"

Let's recap by referring to a short checklist, just to make sure:

	Considered?	Aware?	Plan?			Considered?	Aware?	Plan?
Value Hierarchy					Impacts of Stress			
Financial Beliefs					Resilience			
Limiting Beliefs					Mind Body Relationship			
Psychology			**I**	**It**	**Physical**			
Relationship With Others			**We**	**Its**	**Environment**			
Family					Current work			
Support Network					Financial Setup			
Partnerships					Cultural Expectations			

So, are you ready to make a decision??

Well, before you do that, I want to make sure that you really understand that either decision is perfect.

Business ownership is not for everyone, and there are so many reasons why that is the case, and each and every one of those reasons is valid. If this is not the right path or step (at this moment in time) that does not mean you have to settle for where you are – there are other things to look at – career moves, changing in ways of working etc.…

Business ownership is only one path, one route to the dream reality you want, but it has to be the right path for you. Otherwise you will be opening yourself up to a future that will not be the one you want, and along the way you will encounter stress that will impact on your body, mind, relationships, bank balance and so much more.

You need to be sure. If you're not sure, then go back and re-read the quadrant where you don't feel you can honestly, hand on heart, tick the 'considered', 'aware' and 'plan' boxes with 100% integrity.

So, drum roll please, it's answer time…

"Am I ready and able to be a successful business owner?"

At this point the book splits. If your gut, heart and head answer to the question is a resounding 'yes', then please continue from here. If the answer to that is a considered 'no', then jump to the No section

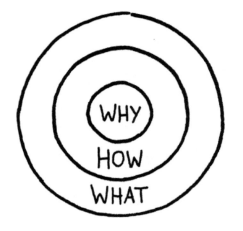

YES, I AM READY TO START MY BUSINESS OWNER JOURNEY...

Well that is awesome news! To get things rolling, I want to share with you a real game-changer about human physiology and how you can use it if you start your business ownership journey from the most powerful place – from within yourself.

THE PHYSIOLOGY OF AN INSPIRED VISION

Business owners who communicate their purpose or cause first, communicate in a way that drives decision-making and action. Based on human physiology, this literally taps the part of the brain that inspires people to take action. As the owner of a business you are responsible for setting the mission (inspiration) that will drive your business' success.

"If you are stuck, and don't feel that your business is moving forward, 99 times out of 100, it's down to a lack of clarity regarding the vision for the business."

- ***Simon Sinek***

THE SCIENCE

Simon Sinek is great at explaining why the 'Why' is so important, he does this using his 'Golden Circle'[21]. He explains that most business communicate from the outside in – starting with WHAT they do, some getting into the HOW they do it, but only the truly successful start from the inside out – starting with the WHY.

WHY is a purpose, a cause or a belief. It provides a clear answer to WHY we get out of bed in the morning, WHY the business exists and WHY that should matter to anybody. Making money is NEVER a WHY - profits, salaries or any monetary measure is simply a result of what we do. The WHY is what inspires us.

People's natural tendency is to think we communicate from the outside in, going from the clearest to the fuzziest. We tell people WHAT we do, we tell them HOW we are different or special and then we expect behaviours, such as purchasing, voting or support, to follow.

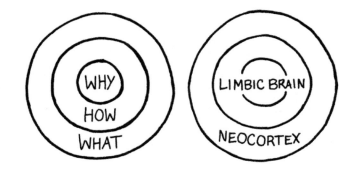

The problem, from a physiological point of view, is that WHAT and HOW do not inspire action. Facts and figures make rational sense, but we do not make decisions purely based on facts and figures. Starting with WHAT is what commodities do. Starting with WHY is what leaders do. Leaders inspire.

It's all grounded in the tenets of biology. If you look at a cross-section of the human brain, what you see is that it is actually laid out in three major components that correlate perfectly with Sinek's Golden Circle.

Our neo-cortex corresponds with the WHAT level. This part of our brain is responsible for all of our rational and analytical thought and language. The middle two sections make up our limbic brain, which is responsible for all of our feelings, like trust and loyalty. It's also responsible for all human behaviour, all decision-making, and it has no capacity for language.

WATCH

Simon Sinek explains this so well, so I suggest you go watch his video to get this from the master himself [22]: *(available via the resources page on iaay.uk/resources)*

RELATING THIS TO BUSINESS

When businesses communicate from the outside in, though people can understand vast amounts of complicated information like features, benefits, facts and figures, it does not drive behaviour.

When businesses communicate from the inside out, they are talking directly to the part of the brain that controls behaviour and decision-making. Then people can rationalise their decision with all the information processed in the neo-cortex. The neo-cortex, (the thinking part of the brain) is always trying to understand and make sense of the world. This is the reason we think we're rational beings when really we're not. If we were, we would never buy a product or service simply because of how it makes us feel. We would never be loyal;

we'd always just choose the best deal. We'd never care about trust; we'd only evaluate the numbers.

But we don't do that.

We do choose one product, service or business over another because we *feel* we can trust them more. We do buy things that we think are worth paying the extra money for even though all the facts and figures may indicate there is no significant difference with the cheaper model.

> *"People don't buy WHAT you do, they buy WHY you do it and what you do simply serves as the tangible proof of what you believe."*
>
> *– Simon Sinek*

When we study businesses that are thriving today, we can see they have this in common: They have clarity of WHY before they moved onto the discipline of HOW and consistency of WHAT. When we dig a bit further, we see that the business owner made the effort to get their own clarity before they could translate that to their business.

So what I want you to do, as the last step in this book, is to articulate your why. To do that we are going to do three exercises together to help you really get down to why you are doing what you're doing, where that came from, and why it will be as inspirationally important to you as it will be to your customers.

ARTICULATE YOUR WHY

There are many articulations of this concept out there - people talking about wanting the life of their dreams, of the job that doesn't feel like work, quotes like: 'love what you do, do what you love, or "follow your bliss", or "Don't ask what the world needs. Ask what makes you come alive and do that... Because what the world really needs is people who have come alive" – they are all talking of the same thing...

Within development circles it's referred to as 'unique ability' (Dan Sullivan), or 'The Hedgehog Concept' (Jim Collins), but the one I like the best (as it suits my eastern spiritual home) is the Japanese 'Ikigai'.

*"**iki** referring to life, and*

gai, which roughly means the realisation of what one expects and hopes for... "

According to the Japanese [23], everyone has an ikigai. Finding it requires an inward looking honesty of self. I think that's why it's so elusive for many people, we are too dominated by superficial things and busy comparing ourselves to others.

Such a search, I believe, is very important since it is believed that discovery of one's ikigai brings satisfaction and meaning to life.

Ikigai is the convergence of four primary elements:

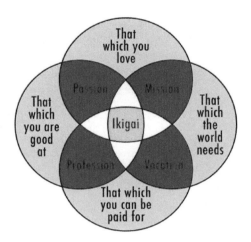

➤ **What you love (your passion)**
➤ **What the world needs (your mission)**
➤ **What you are good at (your vocation)**
➤ **What you can get paid for (your profession)**

Ikigai is the space in the middle of these four elements, and a source of value or what makes one's life truly worthwhile.

WATCH

I really like this TED talk by Dan Buettner [24]; he talks about the impact of ikigai on health and well-being. *(access via the resources page – iaay.uk/resources)*

WHERE DO YOUR CIRCLES INTERCEPT?

In order to articulate your Ikigai, there are four steps to work through, and I've made a templated process to help you. Click to download the worksheets (or if you'd prefer you can make your own) and then read the instructions that follow. To bring the process to love, I've included photos of me doing the process.

Complete Your Ikigai Worksheets

The exercise is available from the iaay website—you need to download the exercises: iaay.uk/resources

On each of the four sheets, within the circles drawn, take some time to brainstorm answers to the questions. Don't worry about how well you phrase the list – just get as many views and ideas out of your head as possible.

- *What do you love?* What aspects of your life bring you into your heart and make you come alive? What do you feel really happy about in your life right now, what energies and excites you?

- *What are you great at?* What unique skills do you have that come most naturally to you? What talents have you cultivated and what do you excel at even when you aren't trying? What great results have you achieved in the past? What sort of skills do you have?

- *What cause do you believe in?* What breaks your heart or pulls at your gut? What change would you most love to create in the world? What would you give your life for? What can you talk about at the drop of a hat, and always get impassioned about?

- *What are you so good at that others ask you for help?* What do people value in you? What service, value or offering do you bring, or could you bring, that brings real value to others? Something people need and are happy to pay for, or share some value in exchange?

STEP 2: CREATING THE FIRST ROUND OF CIRCLES

Cut out the circles that you've written answers in and places them within the map direction on the ikigai map provided

STEP 3: PLOTTING THE FIRST LEVEL OF OVERLAPS

Now take your ikigai diagram and start moving your circles from the outer layer into the overlap areas.

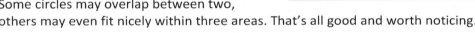

Reflect on the words and explore how these elements may relate to each other and place them into the overlap areas.

Some circles may overlap between two, others may even fit nicely within three areas. That's all good and worth noticing.

Note down any trends and patterns. See where you are naturally being drawn, which words, sentences and emotions are most significant to you?

STEP 4: YOUR IKIGAI

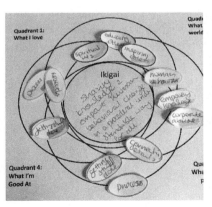

Spend time looking at where your circles have ended up being placed, how do you honestly feel about what you discovered and the overlaps? Is there anything that is sitting uncomfortably, or anything you feel is missing?

When you're ready, bring your attention to the centre of the circles and leave space in your mind for whatever impulse or calling may emerge naturally, that combines all that you've articulated...

THAT IS YOUR IKIGAI....

Having your Ikigai is incredibly powerful.

Now that you have yours, it can act as a guiding star as you move forward – every time you come to a decision point you can assess if it is in line with your Ikigai or helps fulfil your Ikigai.

WHERE DID YOUR WHY COME FROM?

Having done this with hundreds of business owners, I have found time and time again is that when it comes to looking for the origin of the 'why', more often than not, we are looking for a paradox.

Why a paradox? Well, you've just completed an exercise that helps you determine your most basic reason for living. The thing that is most important to you. The word important means we want to *'import it into our sphere of awareness and into our lives'* [25], which ultimately means that we think it is currently missing or void.

Your perceived voids therefore dictate your purpose in life. If someone thinks money is absent from their lives, they search for money. If they think they don't have health, they search for health. Whatever they perceive as missing becomes important.

So in order to understand why your ikigai is what is it, we have to go back and find how the void shaped the 'why', and how that created the purpose. In my experience, if you look back over your life journey you will be able to see two or three major obstacles that you have had to overcome - even master - and this helps you find the origin of your WHY YOU DO WHAT YOU DO.

If we focus on those two or three obstacles and examine what happened, and if we explore how those things in fact benefitted you (by which we mean, what wisdom, insight and motivation was sparked by dealing with those obstacles), resulting in you being, doing and having who and what you are today, we will start to unravel the underlying motivations that are usually left in an unconscious state. Often it is the hardest of times which, while very challenging, help us to grow and afford us the opportunities to make the biggest positive impact on our own lives and of those around us. To fully understand how these times have helped us to grow, we must look beyond the drawbacks and see the benefits.

Exploring the 'schooling' that life afforded us reveals that the biggest obstacles we overcame are precisely what now qualifies us to be masters in these same areas. We feel connected to certain types of people or feel invested in making changes in specific situations that lead to, or are tied to, these two or three obstacles. We will find patterns and trends with values and experiences that create 'a-ha' moments that enable you, as a business owner, to really connect with your business, your employees and your customers in ways you never before thought possible. In ways that are energising, fulfilling, fun and deeply satisfying.

It makes you live with integrity; by which I mean: when who you are on the inside is evident on the outside.

When you align the personal with professional, in this way, something quite extraordinary happens. Your neural physiology changes in a way that encourages you to keep forging ahead so you can more easily build your business.

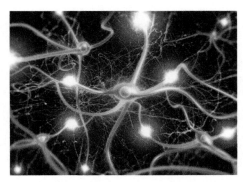

It's called Hebbe's Law [26] and is a basic tenant of quantum physics; neurons that fire together, wire together.

So if you're ready, let's do an exercise to start the discovery process for uncovering where your WHY came from...

YOUR WHY STORY EXERCISE

As before if you'd like to complete this within the Exercise section of this book you will find this there, or you can use your journal.

Typically, your greatest challenges in life are the schooling you need to master the things that give you purpose, persistence, and passion. These challenging experiences often create a void in us that trigger a deep purpose to avoid, prevent, fix, and/or change as a means of filling that void. This tends to be at a completely unconscious level, but once you can reveal and connect to it, the power it gives you is immense.

PART 1:

So let's start by looking at your life from a number of angles, to see if we can identify a pattern or trend that will lead us to your void.

What do you consider to be the major obstacles that you have overcame in your life?

- *What happened?*
- *Who was involved?*
- *What was the impact this had on each person involved?*
- *What does it mean to you that you overcame this? What did it teach you?*

1) What significant experiences have you had in your life that had a big impact on you? (Positive or negative.)

2) Were there any significant experiences that happened to a person close to you, that had a major impact on you? (Your parents, close friend, child, partner etc)

3) What do you have an insatiable curiosity about; what are you obsessed with? Be that knowing, changing, making, building, figuring out, doing, having, being...

4) What is common to each of these answers? Where is the paradox in these people, places or situations? (What were the consequent benefits - what did you learn, who did you meet, what did you experience because of these obstacles?)

PART 2:

Nearly all business owners who start a business because of a specific idea they have, or an inner drive to change the world, can tell the background to that decision. There is usually a catalyst or a trigger, and often it's a great part of their WHY story.

So once again in your exercises section of this book or Journal answer these questions:

1) So what was it (good or bad) that took place and set you thinking about how you could offer a solution?

2) Articulate the specific drivers that pushed you into your current position thinking about becoming a business owner?

3) What was your reason for thinking about setting up this business you have in mind in particular (the name, the type of company, the initial focus)?

4) Who do you want to serve?

5) What problems do you want to solve?

6) What is the vision?

7) Which two or three types of people embody that experience?
   (From now we will call these <people>)

8) What are the three greatest outputs (using this generic term to reflect the full range of things that you could describe here, such as experiences, changes, benefits, etc.) you want to create for your *<people>*?

==========

Having a true understanding of your ikigai and the experiences that caused the void that created it, stands you miles apart from so many other business owners. You are now armed with the ability to make decisions from a truly powerful place. A framework within which to review your choices, assess the insight, advice and recommendations made to you, and make clear, concise and conscious choices that will move you and your business towards these well-articulated ends. It also means you now have the basis on which to truly connect with your business, through the people you hire and the customers you want and will work with you.

There is one final piece I want to add to this puzzle. There will be challenges, which will be many and varied. You will doubt yourself, you will feel overwhelmed at times, question yourself, question all the work you've done here… So it is essential that the WHY you have is big enough to outweigh and override those challenges and obstacles.

YOU MUST HAVE A BIG ENOUGH WHY

The way the brain works, we have a natural built-in resistance to being motivated due to the diminishing return we receive with each small achievement. This means that there is a tendency towards inertia. Inertia can take on many forms, but the main two that are relevant here are:

- ➢ Stagnation – where you do not have sufficient challenge in your life. Growth is always a result of challenge – be that internally or externally provided.
- ➢ Plateau - due to immediate gratification where you are satisfying your material needs only and that causes you to put off growth.

To help this make sense in context, we'll use money as an example, as more often than not that's the way we measure our success and achievement levels.

If you have £1, then earning another £1 is 100% of the value. If you have £10, then another £1 is only 10% and so on:

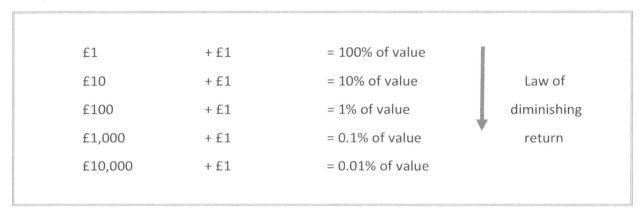

£1	+ £1	= 100% of value	
£10	+ £1	= 10% of value	Law of
£100	+ £1	= 1% of value	diminishing
£1,000	+ £1	= 0.1% of value	return
£10,000	+ £1	= 0.01% of value	

Therefore, the value of earning £1 more becomes less as your wealth increases. So unless you have a cause/purpose that goes up in at least proportion to balance the inertia, you will stagnate and plateau. Working for more money becomes less important, your values are fulfilled enough to make you feel comfortable and therefore your sense of drive slackens and procrastination sets in. I'm sure you've all experienced that feeling.

Your cause/purpose, or the WHY of your business must therefore continue to grow in order to outweigh the depreciation caused by the challenges and obstacles that will come your way. Let's be clear here, there is never a lack of money or success or achievement in the world, only a lack of motivation. If your WHY is big enough, then no challenge can dent that motivation, and the how will take care of itself.

This is also the case when it comes to the diminishing returns of success. We've said that everyone's end goal is different, not everyone wants world domination or to be the market leader or number one in their field. Not everyone wants to be a millionaire – but whatever your target is, as you get closer to hitting it, the law of diminishing returns will set in there too. So to avoid plateauing <u>before</u> you get there, you still need a great big WHY.

"Unless you have a cause bigger than yourself you won't get beyond yourself."

Dr John Demartini

==========

Continuing with the financial area of life as a representative for all areas, we are going to explore what you want the financial output of your business efforts to be, and what you intend to do with that wealth. So these are much more tangible examples, such as:

➢ Paying for the education of your grandchildren and great-grandchildren
➢ Purchasing property
➢ Enabling travel
➢ To retire and sail around the world
➢ Philanthropic contributions to cancer/ animal/ children charities
➢ Leaving a legacy

There are many things that wealth can give you (plus lots it can't), but for the purpose of this exercise we need to ensure that what you are aiming for in the financial area of your life is big enough to overcome that inertia as your business grows or plateaus and/or is challenged.

Use the space in the exercise section of this book or in your journal to jot down your list; really challenge yourself as to whether those targets are really going to push you through the plateau of immediate gratification or the stagnation as a result of obstacles encountered.

============

SUMMARY

As we draw this book to a close, I want you to reflect on what you've achieved. We have done a huge amount of work, I've thrown a lot of exercises, theories and knowledge at you.

Merely the fact that you have reached the end of the book is a reflection of your commitment to yourself and your determination; let's face it, we have all started a book, or an online course, and then been distracted by other things and not finished it. That you have made the time and effort to continue working through this book demonstrates your commitment, and this is another clue that you are on the right track with wishing to pursue business ownership.

So let's refresh. You now have:

➢ Clarity of your suitability for being a business owner;
➢ An understanding of how 'starting with you' allows you to create a framework that is integral to the success of your business plan;
➢ Learnt the basics of integral theory and the importance of having all four quadrants aligned;
➢ Completed practical exercises to exorcise any psychological blockers around abundance, success, money and capability;

- Learnt some new tools to help you manifest all you have learnt throughout your business, along with the means to refresh and maintain it;
- An understanding of what your personal value hierarchy, career anchors and behavioural profile are, and how that manifests in you as a business owner;
- Articulated your ikigai and understood where that came from so that you can make better decisions, ones that will take you faster towards your goals;
- An appreciation of the challenges ahead, how you may want to overcome them and how your WHY needs to be big enough to withstand the road ahead.

That is a lot, and you should be proud of the honesty that you have put into making the most of this book. Very few business owners have this level of insight, clarity and articulation at this stage of their journey. You are now well placed to move forward and look at the idea that has been burning inside of you and assess if it is capable of becoming the business you want to own and run, delivering for you on that WHY in a way that meets your hopes and desires.

NO, I AM NOT READY TO START MY BUSINESS OWNER JOURNEY…

NO, I REALISE NOW THAT BUSINESS OWNERSHIP IS NOT FOR ME …

I'm really proud of you for being brave enough to make one of these statements. If it is the right answer for you right now, then wow, isn't it better to know that than to have moved ahead with that project and experienced the stress and potential disappointment or sense of failure?

I am going to hazard a guess that if you were considering starting a business, that means there is something about your existing career path, specific job or lifestyle, that is not fulfilling or satisfying to you.

What is great though, is that knowing starting a business isn't for you, doesn't mean that your options for altering or addressing those issues stops here. The exercises that you have completed in this book are also a great foundation from which to assess other options.

YOUR CAREER ANCHOR

Understanding what drives your career decisions is helpful. So I would suggest you look at the company you currently work for and reflect on how aligned its vision, purpose and culture is to your anchor. Is it a company that bases itself on service, or on innovation? Does it have a culture of good management? Does it look after the staff well and respect them?

It may well be that the current role you do is a good fit for your interests, experiences and skills, but that the company you're doing it for is not the correct alignment for you at a more fundamental level. I've always said that how you are treated and who you work with is by and large more important than what you do. If you're going to spend 35+ hours a week there, you need to be in a place that you like being in. If that alignment is not there, then maybe a sideways move is actually more appropriate than a whole new start.

YOUR BEHAVIOURAL PROFILE

In the behavioural profile exercise, we looked at an example profile for a business owner, so using the same sort of model to reflect on where you are and where you want to be may be useful.

So why not create a reference profile that you feel best reflects your current job, and see how that relates to the personal profile you created. Explore the gaps by talking to your boss about how you could develop the role you're in to better serve your natural skillset.

Or take some time to reflect on your own profile, and think about what areas your ideal role would require, and take proactive action to develop those skills in yourself – read books, do an online or night class, attend a conference, whatever you can to prepare yourself from a content or skillset perspective.

YOUR VALUE HIERARCHY

Now that you have your value hierarchy, where does work come in that list? Does it really feature? Do you want it to? You can use your value hierarchy to help you improve your current job satisfaction by aligning your work tasks to your values.

=========

EXERCISE: VALUES AND JOB ALIGNMENT

Firstly, let us get clear; please turn to your exercise section of this book, or grab you journal and write down your top three values, and also the three things you dislike the most that you have to do in your current job (which are the source of your job dissatisfaction).

Now, for each of those tasks you dislike, we are going to be open-minded and explore how each task actually helps serve the values you listed. We will then reflect on what the drawbacks would be if that task didn't exist. By doing this you will find four great positives for each task you listed and that will alter your perception at the neural level in your brain.

The four questions I want you to answer against each task are:

1. How does this task serve your highest value?

2. How does this task serve your 2nd highest value?

3. How does this task serve your 3rd highest value?

4. What would be the drawback to your 3 top values if you didn't do this task?

=========

MOVING FORWARD

At this stage it gets really personal, and as this book isn't about career guidance, I am going to stop here.

CONCLUSION

Wow, haven't we been on a great journey together?!? The insight you now have about yourself and what makes you tick, is priceless. As we now draw this book to a close, let's take a little time to reflect on what you've done, what you've learnt and how that prepares you for the next step in your business ownership journey.

You've gained clarity on what the role and responsibilities of a business owner are.

You now know your career anchor and behavioural profile, and how these are so important to know and to consider in your business setup and the role you play within your business.

You've learnt a part of integral theory, and used it to assess your preparedness in all four of the quadrants:

> In **Psychology,** you explored your value hierarchy, your financial mind-set and addressed your self-limiting beliefs.
> In Physical, you explored stress and learnt about resilience and how to improve it. We looked at the relationship between mind and body, and how to get yourself in the best shape for success.
> In Environment, we burst some myths and looked realistically at your financial position and whether you jump or work in parallel; and
> In Relationship with Others we ensured you don't approach this journey as an island, by looking at your family and support networks and how they need to be involved.

You then made a decision as to whether you are ready and able to be a successful business owner.

You chose 'Yes' and then you went on to understand the importance, at this early stage of your journey, to be aware of and able to articulate your WHY. We explored why it is so important for you to be able to explain your why – how that relates to integrity and to enabling your customers to relate to you.

You then did a couple of exercises to articulate your WHY (or Ikigai) and to ensure that you really get how big that WHY needs to be in order to help you overcome the blocks and mountains that will come in your business ownership path.

I understand that for some of you, completing this book is enough for what you currently require. I want to thank you for taking this journey with It's All About You, I hope this book has helped you to further understand yourself and to clarify your business requirements, so you can move forward with a detailed vision that will assist you in making conscious choices that reflect your unique offering to the world.

I really hope you have enjoyed getting to know this side of yourself, and have found the exercises and approach taken in 'It's All About You' useful, relevant and interesting. I would love to hear any feedback and comments at charlotte@consciousaction.co.uk

REFERENCES

Part 1:

(1) http://www.investopedia.com/articles/investing/092514/entrepreneur-vs-small-business-owner-defined.asp#ixzz4poVl67BM

(2) https://www.verywell.com/the-big-five-personality-dimensions-2795422

(3) https://www.youtube.com/watch?v=DmKsDNWs-WQ

(4) http://www.getfeedback.net/hrmanagers/The-Schroder-High-Performance-Managerial-Competencies-framework/ or https://www.youtube.com/watch?v=bEF3GMjmqlk

(5) http://scholar.google.co.uk/scholar_url?url=http://www.its.fsu.edu/sites/g/files/imported/storage/original/application/9046706bf883d41b6d66df0dfa94924a.doc&hl=en&sa=X&scisig=AAGBfm1u8ICsVCJvMGCneGygmXh7tFp8zw&nossl=1&oi=scholarr&ved=0ahUKEwjmuuz36P_WAhXILFAKHXx-DYIQgAMIJygAMAA or http://changingminds.org/explanations/values/career_anchors.htm

Part 2:

(6) http://www.kenwilber.com/Writings/PDF/IntroductiontotheIntegralApproach_GENERAL_2005_NN.pdf or https://integrallife.com/five-elements-aqal/

(7) https://drdemartini.com/

(8) https://drdemartini.com/values/login

(9) https://www.thesecret.tv/products/the-magic-book/

(10) http://annemtheriault.com/tag/law-of-abundance/

(11) https://www.mindtools.com/pages/article/newTCS_82.htm

(12) https://www.dartmouth.edu/~eap/abcstress2.pdf

(13) https://www.heartmath.org/

(14) http://www.sciencedirect.com/science/article/pii/S0883902616300088

(15) http://www.businessinsider.com/10-super-successful-co-founders-and-why-their-partnerships-worked-2010-7?op=1&IR=T

(16) http://www.nytimes.com/allbusiness/AB4113314_primary.html and https://www.business.tas.gov.au/starting-a-business/choosing-a-business-structure-intro/partnership-advantages-and-disadvantages

(17) https://www.entrepreneur.com/article/227576

(18) https://www.nibusinessinfo.co.uk/content/types-joint-venture

(19) http://www.accelerationpartners.com/blog/affiliate-marketing-101-part-i

(20) http://money.cnn.com/2013/01/09/pf/multilevel-marketing-industry/index.html and http://www.businessopportunityplus.co.uk/can-afford-miss-business-opportunity/

Part 3:

(21) https://startwithwhy.com/

(22) https://www.ted.com/talks/simon_sinek_how_great_leaders_inspire_action

(23) http://upliftconnect.com/ikigai-finding-your-reason-for-being/

(24) https://www.youtube.com/watch?v=ff40YiMmVkU

(25) https://drdemartini.com/downloadfile.php?id=473

(26) https://imduk.org/tag/hebbs-law/

(27) https://drdemartini.com/programs/secrets_to_financial_success

IT'S ALL ABOUT YOU – WRITTEN EXERCISES

TABLE OF CONTENTS

Quadrant 1: Psychology/ "I"

Your Why

Addressing a No

EXERCISE - IDENTIFYING YOUR VALUES?

STEP ONE:

Answer the following 10 questions, with 3 examples for each. For each question, chose the three examples that are most important to you. Long sentences explaining yourself is not necessary, this is just for you.

11. How do you fill your personal space?

Look around your home or office, do you see family photos, sports trophies, business awards, books? Do you see beautiful objects, comfortable furniture for friends to sit on, or souvenirs of favourite places you've visited? Perhaps your space is full of games, puzzles, DVDs, CDs, or other forms of entertainment? Do you have books, files and notebooks full of study material? Do you have books and products relating to health enhancement? When you look in your bag, what items do you consistently carry with you as you don't like to leave the house without them?

Whatever you see around you is a very strong clue as to what you value most. So what three things in your space represent you most?

1.

2.

3.

12. How do you spend your time?

You make time for things that are really important to you, and run out of time for things that aren't. Even though people usually say, "I don't have time for what I really want to do", the truth is that they are too busy doing what is truly important to them. You find time for things that are really important to you; somehow, you figure it out. So how do you spend your time? Which three actions do you spend your time on most?

I.e. Checking out the gossip on Facebook (you can put it down as passive socialising if you want); playing games on your phone; listening to music; studying; going to the gym; travelling; watching films; shopping.

1.

2.

3.

13. How do you spend your energy?

You have energy for the things that inspire you – the things you value most – whilst you run out of energy for things that do not inspire you. That's because things that are low among your values drain you, whereas things that are high among your values energise you. In fact, when you are doing something that you value highly, you have more energy afterwards than when you started because you're doing something that you love and are inspired by. Maybe you love to play football so much that you feel energised after the game even if you're tired. So which three activities do you get your energy from?

I.e. Playing cards with your mates right into the early morning; making that big sale come through on the job; working on your motorbike; cycling around Hyde Park; attending a workshop to learn about fitness; planning your holidays

1.

2.

3.

14. How do you spend your money?

Again, you find money for things that are valuable to you, but you don't want to part with money for things that are not important to you. So your choices about spending money tell you a great deal about what you value most. These can be experiences, objects, and services, anything really. What are the three items you spend most of your money on and always find money for?

I.e. Hiring a cleaner because you don't get dirty to be clean; the best headphones because you're an audiophile; sky-diving through the Swiss Alps. Come on, do you really need examples for this one?

1.

2.

3.

15. Where do you have the most order and organisation?

We bring order and organisation to things that are important to us, and allow chaos and disorder to rein in relation to things that are low on our values. It could be your social calendar, your dietary regimen, your clothes and wardrobe, your business, your finances, your spiritual rituals, your cooking area, or your house. Everyone has some item or area of life that is most organised. Which three items or areas do you have most organisation in?

1.

2.

3.

16. Where are you most reliable, disciplined and focused?

You don't have to be prodded from the outside to do things that you value the most; you are inspired from within to do these things and so you do them. Look at the activities, relationships, and goals for which you are disciplined, reliable and focused – the things that nobody has to get at you to do. Which three activities are you most reliable or disciplined at doing?

1.

2.

3.

17. What are your internal dialogue topics?

What do you keep talking to yourself about the most? Not negative self-talk. What you think to yourself about what you desire – internal dialogues that actually seem to be coming true. Which three outcomes about how you would love your life to be do you talk to yourself about most?

For example, your internal dialogue about that dream holiday – that you're researching for, or the relationship that you know you are going to have one day. Or that by the end of the year you will be debt-free.

1.

2.

3.

18. What do you talk about in social settings?

Now here's a clue that you'll probably notice for other people as well as yourself. What are the topics that you keep wanting to bring into conversations that nobody has to remind you to talk about? What subjects turn you into an instant extravert? Topics that immediately bring you to life and start you talking. You can use the same insight to analyse other people's values. If someone asks you about your kids, that means that either their kids or your kids are important to them. If they say, "How's business?" they value business. If they ask, "Are you seeing anyone new?" then relationships matter to them. Topics that attract you are a key indicator of what you value. Which three topics do you keep wanting to talk to others about most?

1.

2.

3.

19. What inspires you?

What inspires you now? What has inspired you in the past? Who inspires you? What is common to the people that inspire you? Figuring out what inspires you most reveals what you value most. Which three people, actions or outcomes inspire you most, and what is common to them?

1.

2.

3.

20. What are the most consistent long term goals you have set?

What are the three long-term goals, that you have been focussing on, that you are bringing into reality? Again, we're not talking about fantasies here. We want the dreams you are bringing into reality, slowly but surely, the dreams that have been dominating your mind and your thoughts for a while. So which are the three most important goals that you keep focussing on, that are gradually coming true and you have evidence of happening.

I.e. To be financially comfortable enough to work part-time; to design and market technology that will be bigger than the iPhone; to write a book; to become a public speaker; to own a range of properties; to climb to Everest Base Camp now and at the age of 65 (unless your 65 now, then this is awkward).

1.

2.

3.

STEP TWO:

Now that you three answers to each of the 10 questions, it's time to identify the answers that repeat most often.

You'll have noticed that among your 30 answers there is a certain amount of repetition (maybe even a lot of repetition) You are expressing the same kinds of values in different ways – for example *"Spending time with people I like", "having a drink with my work colleagues", "Going out to eat with my friends"* – if you look closely you'll see patterns begin to emerge.

Look at your answers and assess the answer that is most often repeated and write beside it number of how often it repeats. Then find the second most frequent answers, then the third, and so on, until you have ranked every single answer. This gives you a good primary indicator of what your highest values are, and the hierarchy of them

Summarise and prioritise your values. Based on how often your answers appear and repeat, create a list of your five most important values in priority order, with the most important first...

1

2

3

4

5

EXERCISE - GUILT RELEASER

This may not start out as the easiest of exercises, but having completed the previous ones, you know that the effort will be worth it. So please persist and trust the process.

We all have a list of things that we believe we've screwed up, the things about our past business dealings that we beat ourselves up about. Here are some examples:

➢ *The client we lost*
➢ *The job interview we flunked*
➢ *The job you lost*
➢ *The course you forgot to attend*
➢ *The job you turned down which you later wished you'd taken*
➢ *The report that was late*
➢ *The data that was wrong*
➢ *The risk you took that didn't pay off*
➢ *The bad hire you made*
➢ *The investment that went bad*

They can be big or they can be small. It's not what happened that's important, it's how you feel about it... So start by making a list of them.

Scan over your list again and star the one situation/ example that makes you feel the most guilt, the one that still has the ability to make you feel really bad about yourself, that you still beat yourself up over.

Now taking that example, you're now going drill a little deeper using the table in the exercise section of this book, or your journal:

First re-write the situation/ explanation at the top.

Then you need to think about the situation, firstly from your own point of view, and come up with AT LEAST FIVE benefits that the situation has given to you.

Examples could be:

- *Losing my job meant more time with my family*
- *I learned a lot about investments that meant I made good ones later on*
- *I had to develop my skills as a manager to get the best out of my team*
- *I met a new contact that became an important colleague/client/associate/business partner*
- *Well yes, it was annoying, but the situation did mean that I moved location*
- *I moved company, and actually preferred it at the new one*
- *I made a new friend/contact*
- *I took my career in a different direction*

Once you get into it you'll find benefits in all aspects of your life (the seven areas can be classified as spiritual, mental, physical, social, career, financial, family) if you get stuck, ask about how the situation helped in each of these seven areas.

Once you've done that, move onto and identify AT LEAST FIVE benefits that situation gave to others (either those directly or indirectly involved).

Examples could be:

- *Losing her job meant XXXX moved to one that suited her better*
- *The incorrect data meant the process got changed and money was saved*
- *Your friendship with XXX was saved as you didn't work together anymore*
- *Your kids got to see you more*
- *XXX got to show their knowledge which meant your role evolved to a better place*
-

Again these can be varied and big or small, but the benefits will be there, if you keep looking...

Why at least five? That's how many it will take to dissolve the guilt you feel about the situation. After that listing that many you will start to view it differently, gratitude for the situation will start to emerge. You do not need to stop at five, if you can do more, then do, as the more the merrier on this exercise. You can of course also re-do this for all the examples you came up with – you don't need guilt in your life or your business so purge it using this really simple technique.

If you struggle with this exercise, that's ok – it's a tough one when you first try it. You could ask someone you trust to assist you, or if you'd like to keep it objective, I'm always here to help – see the end for contact details and 121 session fees.

Situation	
How that situation served you	**How that situation served others**
1.	1.
2.	2.
3.	3.
4.	4.
5.	5.
6.	6.
7.	7.
8.	8.
9.	9.
10.	10.

Adapted from Dr. John Demartini's – The secrets of Financial Success

🏛 **BANK OF ABUNDANCE**

DATE TO CASH MONEY

PAY

TO THE ORDER OF

CURRENCY

Security Features Details on back 🔒

The Universe

DATE SIGNED

⑆000000345⑆ 0030020085⑈ 11000⑆

EXERCISE – VALUE LINKING

Dr. Demartini has developed and utilised two very simple techniques to assist you via a combination of understanding the universal laws of gratitude and attraction and the physiology of the human brain.

Within your value hierarchy, if you want to raise any mention of finances – be that financial success, mastery, security or independence, you need to complete the following steps:

STEP ONE:

In the space below, write **200** general benefits of building wealth and saving money, and how it serves you. Yes, you heard that right, two hundred benefits. With each benefit that you write down you are improving and enhancing the association in the brain between values and money, two hundred is chosen because once you get to this point you've become creative, you've explored all seven areas of your life and you will now start to see many more opportunities for this to manifest in your life. Don't allow yourself to become totally consumed by consumerism here. This isn't about just writing down all the things money allows you to buy – spending your money isn't what financial security or independence is about…. (NB this is not an easy task, it often takes days to get it done – just jot them down when they occur to you, but keep going until you get to 200…

STEP TWO:

Now it's time to get specific. In this list write 200 specific benefits of how building wealth will assist you in achieving your top three personal values.

Start by reminding yourself of your top three values (as distinguished in the first exercise):

1.	
2.	
3.	

Now link these. For example, if your top value is your children, then you need to think about how increasing your wealth will support the fulfilment of that value – i.e. education, health, home…

EXERCISE - YOUR WHY STORY

Typically, your greatest challenges in life are the schooling you need to master the things that give you purpose, persistence, and passion. These challenging experiences often create a void in us that trigger a deep purpose to avoid, prevent, fix, and/or change as a means of filling that void. This tends to be at a completely unconscious level, but once you can reveal and connect to it, the power it gives you is immense.

PART 1:

So let's start by looking at your life from a number of angles, to see if we can identify a pattern or trend that will lead us to your void.

What do you consider to be the major obstacles that you have overcame in your life?

- *What happened?*
- *Who was involved?*
- *What was the impact this had on each person involved?*
- *What does it mean to you that you overcame this? What did it teach you?*

What significant experiences have you had in your life that had a big impact on you? (positive or negative)

Were there any significant experiences that happened to a person close to you, that had a major impact on you? (Your parents, close friend, child, partner etc.)

What do you have an insatiable curiosity about; what are you obsessed with? Be that knowing, changing, making, building, figuring out, doing, having, being

What is common to each of these answers? Where is the paradox in these people, places or situations? (What were the consequent benefits - what did you learn, who did you meet, what did you experience because of these obstacles?)

PART 2:

Nearly all business owners who start a business because of a specific idea they have, or an inner drive to change the world, can tell the background to that decision. There is usually a catalyst or a trigger, and often it's a great part of their WHY story.

So what was it (good or bad) that took place and set you thinking about how you could offer a solution?

Articulate the specific drivers that pushed you into your current position thinking about becoming a business owner?

What was your reason for thinking about setting up this business you have in mind in particular (the name, the type of company, the initial focus)?

Who do you want to serve?

What problems do you want to solve?

What is the vision?

What two-three types of people embody that experience?

From now we will call these *<people>*

What are the three greatest outputs (we've used this generic term to reflect the full range of things that you could describe here - experiences, changes, benefits, etc.) you want to create for your *<people>*?

EXERCISE - HOW BIG IS YOUR WHY

Continuing with the financial area of life as a representative for all areas, we are going to explore what you want the financial output of your business efforts to be, and what you intend to do with that wealth. So these are much more tangible examples, such as:

➢ Paying for the education of your grandchildren and great-grandchildren
➢ Purchasing property
➢ Enabling travel
➢ To retire and sail around the world
➢ Philanthropic contributions to cancer/ animal/ children charities
➢ Leaving a legacy

There are many things that wealth can give you (plus lots it can't), but for the purpose of this exercise we need to ensure that what you are aiming for in the financial area of your life is big enough to overcome that inertia as your business grows or plateaus and/or is challenged.

Use the space below to jot down your list; really challenge yourself as to whether those targets are really going to push you through the plateau of immediate gratification or the stagnation as a result of obstacles encountered

Adapted from Dr. John Demartini's – The secrets of Financial Success

EXERCISE – VALUES & JOB ALIGNMENT

Firstly, let us get clear; Complete the table below with your top three values, and also the three things you dislike the most that you have to do in your current job (which are the source of your job dissatisfaction).

	WHAT ARE YOUR 3 TOP VALUES	WHAT ARE YOUR 3 LEAST INSPIRING JOB TASKS
1		
2		
3		

Now, for each of those tasks you dislike, complete the table below by being open-minded and exploring how each task actually helps serve the values you listed. Then reflect on what the drawbacks would be if that task didn't exist. By doing this you will find four great positives for each one, and that alters your perception at the neural level in your brain.

Uninspiring Task	How does this task serve your highest value?	How does this task serve your 2nd highest value?	How does this task serve your 3rd highest value?	What would be the drawback to your 3 top values if you didn't do this task?
Task 1				
Task 2				
Task 3				

This exercise is adapted from Dr John Demartini's 'Demartini Method', which is a scientific process that balances perceptions and emotions

Printed in Great Britain
by Amazon